AWAKENING
the
Lightworker Within

A PERSONAL JOURNEY
OF ANSWERING
THE SACRED CALL

ELIZABETH J. FOLEY

STREET

Angel Street Publishing, LLC
P.O. Box 7298
Nashua, NH 03060

Awakening the Lightworker Within: A Personal Journey of Answering the Sacred Call / Elizabeth J. Foley

ISBN 13: 978-0-9800806-0-5
ISBN 10: 0-9800806-0-6

January 2008

Printed in the United States of America

Contents

AUTHOR'S NOTE

ALL OF THE STORIES contained in this book are true. I have changed the names and identifying details to protect the anonymity of my personal friends, students and clients. The only exception is my own story and where permission was obtained.

When mentioning God, some people prefer synonyms to the name "God" such as Universal Spirit, Beloved Creator, Divine Father-Mother. Whatever your belief system is or how you refer to God, if you feel more comfortable in substituting these other names for God, please do so.

FOREWORD

I S IT POSSIBLE THAT we are here for a grander purpose? Perhaps it's one that hides from us like some elusive shadow... ghost-like thoughts that dance around us and poke us with intuition that tells us so... then back away quickly, making us wonder if we were dreaming or not, like a game being played with our consciousness.

The premise is a metaphysical one. Metaphysics means "beyond physics," or more commonly, "beyond our recognized reality." With free choice we live our lives the best we can, given the culture we live in and the challenges we create as we go. Could it be, however, that under the surface of what we perceive to be our reality, there is another? Many of us believe this to be so. We receive hints along the way to "look beyond the veil." Often, it frightens us. Sometimes we create fears that keep us from looking, and many times we simply ignore it all as fairly simple self talk. But what if the whole premise was true? What if free choice calls us to something bigger than we have been told is there?

The term Lightworker has been defined as one who has

recognized the challenge of finding this new truth, and is actively working this grand puzzle. For what is before this person is the task of recognizing the "system of how things work." At the outset it appears to be chaotic, not logical, out of 3D, and random. But as you begin to search within, you realize that it is real. You find it's huge, perfect, loving, empowering, and something that slowly has an odd symmetry about it.

Elizabeth's story is laid out for you to see how this works. It's not just for you to admire Elizabeth on her journey. The entire purpose of the book is for you to see yourself in her, and look at the synchronicity of her journey compared to yours. Perhaps you didn't meet an angel who saved your life when you were 22, but were there some other things that made you wonder about "fate?" We all get them, as an invitation to begin to "look around" and see what might be inside us all.

Elizabeth discovered her divinity. She realized the issues and what to do about them. She had a merger with her Higher-Self and never looked back, and it took her years to do it. What if a book like this helps you work MORE quickly through things that took Elizabeth a very long time within an older energy? What if it's not an accident that you are reading this?

When the elusive ghosts of thought circled around Elizabeth years ago, and whispered in her ear, "You are here for something special," she avoided them for awhile. She even feared them. But then she opened the door wide. Now, all these years later, you are holding that "something special" in your hand. Suddenly, Elizabeth's synchronicity is yours also. Think about it. What a system!

Celebrate events like this that appear significantly related but have no discernible connection, for this is often the way Angels appear to guide you in your life. Celebrate this book!

Lee Carroll - Author of the channeled Kryon book series and "The Indigo Children"

INTRODUCTION

FOR WHAT SEEMS LIKE eons, we-humanity as a whole- have lived in spiritual slumber. Yet as Paramahansa Yogananda once said "The basic You is infinite in its' potentiality."

We do possess great power and have infinite potential to create Heaven on Earth! And as we move into the twenty-first century, there is great cause for optimism and hope.

Today, there are new children, new visionaries and messengers of the Light who are here to assist this spiritual evolution. They are the indigo and crystal children, who hold strong and clear visions of hope for humanity despite the profound challenges that face us now.

Through humanity's group consciousness, people all over are far more spiritual today than they ever have been. More and more people are truly turning to God and realizing they have angels and that they too are magnificent beings of light and love.

Yes! Our long awaited awakening is finally here and it is

wonderful, magnificent and exhilarating...and at the same time it can be scary, frustrating and confusing.

HOW do we do all this 'evolving' day to day and balance it? Where are those angels when we need them and how can we know what God wants for and of us? Are we also Lightworkers- and what does that even mean?

Awakening the Lightworker Within, A Personal Journey of Answering the Sacred Call is about my own spiritual journey. I share with you intimate details of the struggles of my own life and how the Divine-within and through synchronicities-guided and transformed me, an ordinary person, into a Lightworker.

A Lightworker is simply one who agreed on a soul level to be here on planet Earth to help make a difference, whether it is expressed through touching a few souls or working with the multitudes and masses. In truth we are all Lightworkers, here to learn from and teach each other, and to care for the planet.

It is my sincerest hope and aspiration that as you read, your own spiritual truth will become clearer, more attuned to your own bigger purpose and the way the Divine is already at work within your own Life. That at your deepest heart level you will more fully awaken to whom you truly are: a being of great Light with the potential to be all that you aspire to be and to go forth touching other people's lives.

Chapter 1

IN THE COMPANY OF ANGELS

A S I DROVE HOME to New Hampshire from Maine I began thinking about my schedule for the next day. It was around 1:00 AM by the time I got in and feeling very content and yet exhausted, I quickly unpacked my teaching gear, and headed for bed.

I had just taught a class called "Touching the Angelic Realm," which is one of my favorite classes to teach. It was a rather large group, and everyone enjoyed themselves. Lively discussion ensued after the lecture, which was followed by looking at some real angel photos. I always travel with these, many of which are given to me by students and clients. It's quite a collection now, and as a spiritual teacher, I find it valuable to show them. The pictures are validating and do provide some tangible proof that angels or angelic energy is real and does exist.

The class had ended on a positive note, and I could see

that the material discussed had moved some people. I could see their spiritual light bulbs being turned on, for the class itself had stirred up questions and possibilities for many.

Tired yet thankful, I let thoughts of the class and tomorrow's schedule drift away into sleep.

What seemed like only a moment later, the phone rang, but incredibly my clock said 7:00 A.M. I thought, "Who could be calling me this early in the morning?" I jumped out of bed and slowly moved to find the phone. "Hello, Divine Healing," I said with a fuzzy voice.

"Hi Elizabeth, it's Lisa. Did I awaken you?"

"Yes, but that's okay. I taught last night and got in really late. How can I help you?"

"Well, you probably don't remember me, but I have gone to several of your classes."

I searched my memory to try to make a connection, but none came.

"Elizabeth, I am sorry to have awakened you, but I need your help. It's urgent. Do you ever visit people in hospitals?"

Lisa explained that her cousin Pauline was in the hospital in Burlington, Massachusetts, having been diagnosed with Non-Hodgkin's lymphoma. This fatal disease tends to be widespread and involves the growth of malignant tumors.

Lisa continued on, saying she and Pauline had stayed up most of the night discussing treatment strategies and what to do next. It seemed that chemotherapy was the only viable option left. Lisa decided to call in the angels for this one. As Pauline listened to Lisa speak about her guardian angels, her eyes lit up like the sun, feeling hopeful for once. She had never known that she had angels around her, and with excitement in her voice, asked Lisa to do an angel reading for her. Not feeling very comfortable with doing a reading herself, Lisa told Pauline that she knew of someone who could, and she would contact this person right away.

"Elizabeth, could you please come to the hospital today? The doctors want to give Pauline another course of chemotherapy today, but she may end up with her vocal cords being totally paralyzed." Pauline had had a severe reaction to the chemotherapy medications that were administered the day before.

Double checking my schedule and seeing all the appointments booked for that day, I still said yes and told her that I could be there in the early afternoon. I would have to make some phone calls to reschedule people.

Everyone I called was kind and understanding. Before leaving for the hospital, I received some Divine guidance, which was to bring a deck of angel cards with the intent to give them to Pauline. On my arrival, Lisa met me in the waiting room telling me again how excited Pauline was about meeting me and having her angel reading.

Pauline was in her late 60s but looked much older as she lay in the hospital bed with what seemed like every tube and needle known to man connected to her, monitors all around and an oxygen mask on her face. As I walked into the room, she pulled off her oxygen mask and said, "Hello," then asked, "Are you the one who will tell me more about my angels?" Answering "Yes," I looked around. The room seemed really small with all the equipment in there, and it was challenging to find a space where I could lay out my cards and do her reading. Pauline was so excited that she kept pulling off her oxygen mask, causing alarms to go off when she kept it off for too long. She didn't even care, for she just wanted to know more about her angels.

Pauline reminded me of a little child who had just gotten

a wonderful new toy or a new friend. "Elizabeth," Pauline said, "Lisa tells me I have angels. Do I *really* have angels? How many and what are their names? Can you tell me all this?"

The questions kept coming one right after the other. Pauline was so eager to know more and connect with her own angels that sometimes it was hard to get a word in edgewise.

Laughing, I told her "Pauline just relax and calm down and please keep your oxygen mask on!" The nurses were constantly monitoring the equipment and giving her more medication. They didn't seem to care who I was or why I was there, but Pauline told them anyway that I was there to talk to her about her angels.

At first I sat on her bed and spoke to her about angels in general.

"Everyone has guardian angels around them Pauline, and for most, there are usually two. Our guardian angels never leave our side--no matter what happens. They never judge us. They are always there to guard, guide and protect us, and they are beings of pure Divine love. Basically they function as our own personal life coach and cheerleader."

Then we talked about her specific guardian angels that are around her all the time. Her angels, very eager to connect with her, gave me their names of Grace and Joseph. I asked Pauline if she ever saw quick sparks or flashes of white light (especially at night). These lights, I explained, are the energy of the angels that we can see with our physical eye, and are called "angel lights." Pauline said that sometimes she would see them but had not really known what they were. She laughed as she told me she'd thought that there was something wrong with her eyes.

While talking with Pauline about angels, I also spoke

to her about Archangel Raphael, who is noted as the healing angel whose energy is a brilliant emerald green color. I let her know that she could work with Archangel Raphael while she was in the hospital, to have him watch over her and her hospital care, as well as guiding her medical team.

Looking around her hospital room, I was able to find a little stool that I used as a table to lay out the angel cards for her reading. Pauline's eyes glowed with excitement and anticipation for what her angels wanted to tell her. She was thrilled with the information and messages that she received from her angels, and immediately began working with Archangel Raphael for her physical healing.

She also asked Raphael to supervise her medical care and to work with her and her doctors, while watching over her. Later that same day when her physician decided to continue with the chemotherapy despite her adverse reaction of the day before, Pauline was amazed to find that she was able to better tolerate her chemotherapy treatments.

What made her happiest, however was knowing that she was not alone, and just before leaving I was guided by my angels to give her a deck of her own angel cards so that she could have yet another method to communicate with and get messages from her angels.

In the days that followed, Pauline constantly spoke to her guardian angels and Archangel Raphael. She remained positive and hopeful. She now knew that her angels were around her, as she continued to see the angel lights that we had spoken about earlier.

A few weeks later, Lisa let me know that Pauline had passed on. Her healing had been a spiritual one, freed of fear. She died peacefully with a smile on her face and her angel cards in her hands knowing that she was always in the company of angels.

On learning of her passing, I wondered once again, "Who would have thought I could be a Divine messenger for God and the angels?"

Chapter 2

IN THE BEGINNING

MANY TIMES I AM asked in my classes and workshops, "Elizabeth, how did you get started?" or "Did you always feel that you were here for a greater purpose?" or "When did your journey begin?"

Did you ever feel like YOU are here for some greater purpose? Did you ever feel somehow different from everyone else? Well, I did.

I have been told many times by psychics and other spiritual teachers that I am a very old soul. Sometimes I even physically feel that way. However, for the most part, I knew at a young age that I was here to make a difference for God and humanity. I did not have the particular details of my soul mission, but I definitely knew I had some kind of a spiritual path to follow. Only time would tell of the details and the challenges I would face before discovering my path.

My entrance into the world was a precarious one. My mom tells me of my difficult birth, and while I am still not sure exactly what happened just after birth, I do know I was hospitalized for almost 14 months.

The local physician then told my parents that there was nothing more they could do for me, and they handed me over to my parents to either live or die.

The funny thing was, my parents had to feed me some pretty weird stuff just to keep me alive. One thing that I had to drink was popcorn water. Why? I am truly not sure. Mom would make popcorn then soak it in water, and then drain the popcorn and feed it to me. When I now think about this, it sounds awful. From a spiritual perspective, I must have been thinking twice about being here. Someone or my guardian angels must have convinced me to stay so that I could complete my soul purpose and mission.

In 2002 I had the pleasure of meeting a medical intuitive from England named Maggie. She was a very serious and mysterious-looking gal. With her dark hair and eyes, she gave me the feeling that she knew everything about me. It was almost like she could read my soul.

She seemed a beautiful soul with a deep commitment to helping and healing others, so I decided to have a reading with her. She commented on my difficult birth, even though she had no prior conscious knowledge of it. At one point during my session with her, she said that I had died and come back.

No one knew what was wrong with me back then. My mom had only said that I had allergies. Yes, allergies to life, maybe. However, if the same thing happened now with all of our medical knowledge and advances, Maggie felt that I would have been diagnosed with either "Sudden Infant Death Syndrome" (SIDS) or "Failure to Thrive" syndrome.

Maggie recommended doing a past-life regression, but I truly was not interested in reliving this part of my life. I don't remember any of this and maybe it's a good thing not to.

Two other psychics told me almost the same thing, but only one of them attempted to give me more specifics as to what happened at birth. This psychic can read energy and went back to the beginning to unravel the mystery of my birth. Her explanation was that there had been a psychic attack like a negative energy force that wanted possession of my physical body. This sounded really far-fetched, but on some level it made sense to me. Not having any other explanation, I decided that this could be a possibility. I certainly don't remember, but a host of angels must have intervened on my behalf. My perspective now is that no one and nothing had been allowed to interfere with my soul mission.

As a child, I would often play "church," and I was the priest. Pinning my blanket on my shoulders and pretending that it was my robe just like the priests'; I would go through the motions of conducting mass and used potato chips for the communion host. I can laugh at this now, but it all spoke to my soul. My present belief is that I have had some past lives as a priest or a monk or some type of religious leader or teacher.

My first name Elizabeth means "a promise to God," and I made a promise to God a long time ago. I am here to be the spiritual teacher and healer that I was meant to be. During one meditation, I was given a message that said, "You are a rock for others to build their church on."

Shortly after I started teaching about angels and other spiritual matters, I recall getting ready to give a talk to a group of metaphysical students in Salem, Massachusetts. The owner of the store had an aura machine, and I just love playing with this technology. While her students were coming in and getting settled, the owner came up to me and said, "We have a few minutes before we start, would you like to have your aura picture taken?" Well, I did not have to think twice about this and said, "Yes, let's play a little before class."

While she was starting up the aura machine, I quickly finished my preparation for teaching my class on angels and I asked Archangels Michael and Gabriel to work with me. I had invoked Michael to "clear" the students and the area I was going to be in to prepare sacred space for the class. I asked Gabriel to work with me to stay focused on my talk and to open my throat chakra so that I could speak my truth and the information with love and compassion.

I have always trusted that when I asked the angels and my guides to assist me, they do. But today was going to be a very special day for me. I was in for an unexpected treat.

Right away I could see my aura on the computer screen. The colors danced around and then settled in. I could not believe what I saw with my own eyes. A band of golden energy shaped like a hand was moving right into my throat chakra. I often see Archangel Gabriel as a golden energy almost like the sun. I had asked Archangel Gabriel to open my throat chakra for the class, and this was a powerful way to validate that the job was being done!

Next, both the store owner and I had to do a double take. There it was--a white cross over my third eye. We could plainly see it on the computer screen, but on the photo printout it only showed pink energy. I knew the cross on the forehead was very meaningful, though it would be three years before I learned its significance.

According to some spiritual teachers and leaders, those who follow their own spiritual path and practice their own spiritual beliefs and practices are marked with a cross on their forehead. This means that they are a church of God and not of man. Those who are clairvoyant can sometimes see this cross, or some may just have a strong feeling or knowingness that the cross is there.

In looking back over the past five years or so, that meditation message makes perfect sense. With all the spiritual teaching that I do in empowering others, including other Lightworkers, I see myself providing them with a foundation to build on and then keep growing. Even though I work extensively with the angelic realm, I need to be and am very well grounded in my body and in my work.

In the beginning, I knew I was meant to be here for some larger purpose than I could then understand. Again, only time, and the sequence of events and the synchronicity of things to come would tell the story.

Chapter 3

SAVED BY AN ANGEL

I WAS ABOUT 22 YEARS old when I met Mark. He was the friend of my long-time high school friend Dee. I was attracted to Mark and finally decided to talk to Dee about it. He also was attracted to me but was too bashful to even approach me for a date. So Dee acted as the matchmaker and love liaison for us.

We started dating shortly after Dee opened the door, and I learned that Mark was a kind and generous soul. He seemed to like everything that I liked, though later I realized that he was too eager to please me and hence lost his own identity.

While we were still dating, both he and Dee came up with the idea of going canoeing in Maine at Saco Bound. This is a place in Saco, Maine where you can rent a canoe and paddle up or down the Saco River. They give you maps and life preservers and other equipment. Dee and Mark kept bugging me to go, even though I was trying to study for some mid-term exams. I finally gave in, and they made all the arrangements. All I had to do was show up! Saco

Bound was a very popular place, and the only day that they had availability was October 31st, Halloween.

When we left Nashua, New Hampshire the weather was a bit overcast with the temperature around 60 degrees. I bundled up, dressing in layers and my huge and heavy hiking boots. The three of us packed the car with goodies and cameras, and, for some strange reason, Mark packed three extra sets of clothes. So off we drove to Saco, Maine.

As we drove further north, the weather changed somewhat. It was getting colder and windy. By the time we got to our destination, there were totally overcast skies, colder weather and even more wind. We walked into Saco Bound, Mark spoke with the person behind the desk, informing him that we had reservations to go canoeing that day, and paid the fees.

There was only one person working at Saco Bound that day, and he must have told us at least 10 times, "Whatever you do, do not capsize. It's the perfect weather for hypothermia." We all heard him, and what he told us just went in one ear and right out the other. None of us understood what hypothermia was, and at that age 'if you don't know what it is, then don't worry about it' was my motto.

Because this warning was given to us all many times, we should have paid more attention. Yet, we all ignored that warning.

Saco Bound gives you a map, and you tell them which river path you're going to take as well as approximately what time you will arrive at the end point. Then they pick you and your canoe up with the van at the end point. How convenient, I thought. We grabbed our gear, got our map of the river and told the guy that we were going to take the "A" path down the river, which was about a 5-hour canoe ride.

Only our angels knew what was in store for us that day and that it could have been my last day here on planet earth.

It was definitely much colder outside than when we had left Nashua. All the same, we three were all very eager to get going and start having some fun. We crossed the street with the canoe and all of our gear. They had given us life preservers, but none of us used them. I had too many clothes on and I thought that if I were to wear the life preserver, I would not be able to move with all the layering I had. I never checked with Mark and Dee to see if they knew how to swim. I did, and simply assumed they did too. We all know what 'assume' stands for.

Finally we were in the water with the canoe, our paddles, life preservers, food, water, cameras and other stuff. As we paddled down the Saco River, we periodically beached to eat, relax and explore. I love discovering new things! We all acted like big kids, and everything was going great until the weather started to shift and change even more drastically. The temperature began dropping and then it began snowing. It was really cold, and there was no place to stop and get warm. You'd think that with all the layers of clothing I had, I should have been very toasty. That was not the case.

We all took fair turns at paddling. We only had one more mile to go before we would get to the end point. The river itself, for the most part, was shallow, but now in the final stretch, it was getting deeper and had stronger currents.

At one point, Dee was way in the back of the canoe paddling, Mark was sitting in the middle and I was up in front paddling and trying to stay warm. Mark gently tapped me on the shoulder and said that he could take over from here, just hand him the paddle. I gladly did. Now I was still in front all curled up trying to keep warm, and I closed my

15

eyes and was trying to imagine that I was on a nice white sandy beach in Miami, Florida and that the sun was baking down on me. Just a few seconds later, I found myself in the water. We had somehow capsized.

It took me a few seconds to realize what had happened, and still to this day, no one knows exactly how it happened. No one rocked the canoe or even moved. Maybe it was the wind that picked us up.

I was amazed that I surfaced pretty quickly, even with all of my layers of clothes and heavy hiking boots. We all did surface, but very far apart from each other. Normally if I can't feel or especially see the bottom of the water, I panic. I started to panic but then told myself to pull it together and to focus on getting to dry land.

Mark was the closest to me, and together we managed to flip the canoe right side up. We had lost some equipment, but we didn't care. At this point, Dee was hysterically screaming that she didn't know how to swim. She kept screaming of her fear of dying and that her children were not going to have a mother. An awful realization hit Mark and I simultaneously: Dee did not know how to swim and she had no life vest. I shouted back to her to focus on swimming, and told her how to do the dog paddle, a simple swimming technique. She kept screaming that she was going to die and leave behind her young kids.

I told Mark to get the canoe to Dee quickly, that I would be okay on my own because I could swim. I must honestly admit, I did not like being left alone in the middle of the river where I could not feel or see bottom. Talk about working out your fears.

We all got to the riverbank--a little shook-up to say the least, but all okay. At first when I got out of the water, I felt warm and thought, 'All right this was not so bad.' But within seconds I began to shiver uncontrollably. Hypothermia was setting in and I did not even know it.

Mark looked tired, and thankfully Dee was fine but I was freezing and couldn't even really speak too well. My body temperature was dropping fast, and I still did not get the whole picture. We were lost as lost could be. We found an old dirt road with several summer cabins, but summer was over, and the cabins were all closed and locked up for the winter months. We even attempted to break into one of them but could not.

We walked on, heading in the direction that the canoe had been going, but there was no sign of life anywhere. I was getting really tired, could barely speak coherently, and my limbs were numb. I could not feel my legs or hands and my body ached. Dee was just a little cold, and Mark seemed just fine though weary from the whole ordeal. I tried to tell him that I was very sleepy and could not keep my eyes open. Then we came across this huge pine tree and I motioned to him that I was going to lie down for a while to rest while he and Dee could try to find help.

I started to lay my body down next to the tree but he screamed, "No! Get up! You have to stay with us and just keep walking!" He grabbed my arm and kept pulling me along. I tried to fight him to let go of me so that I could sleep for a while. I needed to sleep.

We walked aimlessly for a while longer when we saw a car coming down the road. Mark ran into the middle of the road, waving his hands to flag this person down. I could see the car and it looked like an old chocolate brown color Cadillac. I could not see the person driving the car yet, but I was getting a little nervous thinking, 'Here we are in the middle of nowhere and no one knows what has happened to us.' I kept motioning to Mark to get out of the road and let the car go by. God, what was I thinking? I'll tell you, I was thinking that it was going to be some crazy person with a gun or knife.

Instead, we were in for an encounter with an angel. God only sends his/her very best to help out during times of crisis.

The car slowed down and the driver put down his window. We locked eyes, and they were the bluest eyes I ever had seen. He was an older gentleman with all white hair. Looking at this stranger, I felt like as though I had met him before somewhere. Then I had a flashback to one summer night a couple of years before, when I experienced something very strange.

At the time I was still living at my parents' home. I had fallen asleep quickly, yet in the middle of the night, somewhere between 2 am and 3 am, I was abruptly semi-awakened. My eyes were open and I looked down at my feet and across to the open windows in front of me. Next I looked up and saw a white face. I saw nothing else... no body or wings or really anything else. The face was all white, and this being had the most loving eyes that I ever had seen. Of course, I was scared at the time and even tried to scream but could only make a faint noise. I tried to push this being away, but found that I could not move my arms or body. I was paralyzed but, after a few seconds of trying, I was able to free myself. Then I reached for this face with my hands. The being disappeared. Scared out of my mind, I decided to sleep with the light on for the rest of the night, not knowing what to think of it all.

Now here we were and Mark was trying to tell the driver very quickly what had happened, and this angel spoke ever so softly saying only, "Get in the car. I know what happened." We all sat in the back and soaked his entire seat.

This man kept looking in his rear-view mirror at us and especially kept an eye on me. I am not sure why, but when Mark tried to tell him that we were lost, this angel simply said, "I know where you are going," and never spoke another word to any of us (not even his name). I thought that this was all so very strange. Most strangers would strike up a conversation like, "Hi. What is your name and where are you from? My God, what happened?" But nothing like that happened.

The ride was short but seemed far longer because the driver never engaged us in a conversation. The driver of this car just seemed to know what happened and where exactly to take us. Sure enough, he was right on the money. We arrived at our destination with the Saco Bound person already waiting for us, and we piled out of the car. Mark explained to him what happened, and they both went off to find the canoe, which they did.

I went right to the Saco Bound van and sat in front of the heater. Only seconds had passed between getting out of the car and getting into the van, yet when I looked around for this stranger, both he and his car just seemed to have vanished. No trace was left behind! The sad thing is I could not remember if I had thanked this angel. Now he was gone!

We all returned safe and sound at the Saco Bound site, and the guy said that we should take off our clothes and ring them out a bit. Mark spoke up and said, "I brought with me extra clothes." For some reason, Mark had packed three extra pair of underwear, pants and sweaters. I asked him, "Why three?" and all he said was "I just knew I needed to do that."

When I got back home, I looked up hypothermia in one of my medical dictionaries, and discovered that the need to sleep was a clinical sign that I was going into the fourth stage of hypothermia and what would have followed next was death.

As I said previously, my first name Elizabeth means "a promise to God." I guess I survived because I hadn't yet fulfilled my promise. I am truly grateful for this Divine intervention. Was this purely a stranger helping out, or was it an angel in disguise? I certainly believe that I was visited and saved by an angel. You decide!

MY SPIRAL DOWN

I N THE COURSE OF the many readings I have done,
I have met all kinds of people. Sometimes the people
who come to me reflect back to me the person I used to be
- unhappy and frustrated, and disillusioned with life itself.
Their stories remind me of me. For many years, I lost touch
with myself and felt spiritually blocked. Unable to even
hear my own heart speak to me anymore, I moved from
one job to another. With each new job, I just became more
depressed and even numb. I got to the point where I hated
all of my jobs, my friends, my family and my whole life. I
decided to drown myself in prescription drugs. It seemed
that taking pills was much easier than facing myself.

I was too scared to do street drugs, but prescription
medication seemed safer I assumed. I became a functional
addict, abusing many different types of drugs, mostly in
the antidepressant family. These medications helped me to
cease caring about anything at all: I had started my serious
spiral down. So far down, in fact, that at one point I did not
even care if I lived or died. In fact, death was starting to

look really good. I felt like I had no options. Just what do you do and where do you go when you hate everything and everyone, including yourself?

I sought some help on my own but realized that the therapist I was seeing had more problems than I did. Sometimes the psychotherapy sessions were more about her than me. And do you know what is really amazing? The doctor that I was seeing knew I had an addiction problem and kept prescribing more medications. Now does that make any sense?

By age 28, I was completely depressed. My spiral down had hit rock bottom. I still hated my job, my friends, my family, everyone and everything including myself. I was clearly quite suicidal. I remember my mom being so freaked out that whenever we went somewhere together, she would insist on driving and would lock the doors so that I could not jump out and kill myself.

Finally, at age 29, I decided to hospitalize myself. The psychiatrists at the hospital even put me on some more psychotropic medication. All kidding aside, I felt like I was a walking pharmacy.

Then all of a sudden, at around age 32, I decided I had had enough with addiction. I was tired of having pills control my life and so made a decision to step back into my own power. No more "pity pot" and no more prescription drugs. I decided to just stop everything. Into the garbage my prescription drugs went and I canceled all of my therapy appointments. Cold turkey was the only way to go I believed, and I went and did it! For me, fortunately, it was the right decision.

I truly do not know what happened or what made me make this drastic change, but of course I am very glad I did. Maybe it was the angels trying to help me or a combination of my angels and my higher self working together. Not really sure what happened, but I was lovingly nudged to move along on my spiritual journey. It felt as though my own soul was trying to reach me and to get back on track again. Whatever or whomever it was, I am very grateful for the Divine intervention.

Addictive behavior had also been part of my family experience. My father had a drinking problem and that is how he drowned his sorrows and disappointments. My brother Rick was not too far behind him. Luckily, Rick took some painful steps and started watching his own drinking behavior. Both my father and brother have been sober for years now.

My own prescription addiction had lasted almost 10 years. Once I was back on track, I made a commitment to myself and started taking some action. I applied for better-paying jobs in the health field. Still wanting to make a difference, a global difference, I took a job in clinical research and worked between 1991 and 2002 in some of the biggest pharmaceutical companies in Massachusetts. That is another chapter all in itself.

Chapter 5

CHANGE OF HEART

AFTER GRADUATING FROM COLLEGE in 1982 with a Master's degree in Counseling, I decided to open my private counseling practice, with the goal of saving the world. Now does that sound familiar? I guess I had a real big ego and truly thought I could save the whole world. What was I thinking?

I attempted the private practice route, but no one called me. Still determined to make a difference somehow, I did some counseling work for the state of New Hampshire, working with physically abusive parents. I thought that this was what I could offer. I had some pretty naïve notions about changing people. I slowly discovered I couldn't change anyone but me.

This job affected my very soul. After going through an extensive training program by the State, I thought I could handle just about anything. Well, I was in for quite a surprise.

For the most part, I enjoyed my counseling work and did feel that I was making some kind of a difference to others. I had high hopes of helping families to have a better quality of life. However, all that changed one night.

I was working part-time at a local hospital in the admitting office to help supplement my income. While working, I received a phone call from the emergency room that there was a four-year-old child needing a special set-up in pediatrics. Because there was no pediatric ICU room at this hospital, I needed to page the hospital engineer, who had to create a mini-ICU room for this child. I gave him a list of things needed, and he went to work.

Shortly after, I received another phone call from the emergency room saying that they would be sending the child's mother up to the admitting office and that the police department was going to escort her to my office. While waiting for them to arrive, the hospital engineer stopped by to tell me that everything was in place and ready to go. The mother and two police officers arrived at my door.

The paperwork that accompanied them from the emergency room stated that the admitting diagnosis was "Child Abuse." My heart sank. After finishing the paper work, the police escorted the mother away. I could not visit the child because she was so badly burned. At four years old this child experienced, in my opinion, extreme cruelty from her own mother. Apparently, the child had been crying and the mom could not make her stop. The mother had her live in boyfriend fill the bathtub with boiling hot water and immerse the child in it. The child suffered third-degree burns from the waist down. What a sight and what an experience! How could a mother do this to her child? I could not make any logical sense out of this one.

I'd had enough! My complete change of heart about counseling and human services led me to leave that field altogether. Over the next several years I held various jobs, usually working between two to three jobs to make ends meet and pay off my student loans. The jobs were not satisfying, and my soul still begged to help make a difference--but now I felt stuck.

Still searching for a way to make a real difference in this world, I went back to college to get yet another Master's degree, this time in Public Health, and thought I could serve humanity in this role. While attending graduate school at Boston University School of Medicine, I applied for a clinical research job at the college, working as a research assistant for an Alzheimer's genetic program. Alzheimer's is a horrible neurological disease that can rob a person of his or her identity, and it is painful to see anyone progress with this condition.

Still not sure what direction to go in, I continued in Alzheimer's genetic research after my graduation in 1995. Finally I decided to branch out and tried the private corporate world of pharmaceutical research. I truly thought that if I could help develop a good clinical trial drug study and assist in the process of getting a new medicine to market, that it could help countless number of people. I worked for several large pharmaceutical, biotech and medical device companies in Massachusetts over a period of about eight years. The money was very good, but it still did not totally speak to my soul. I was having yet another change of heart, with no idea of what would come next.

Chapter 6

MY INTRODUCTION TO THE ANGELS

MY 'FORMAL' INTRODUCTION TO the angels did not come with a big brass band. There wasn't a visitation by an angel, nor did I have a near-death experience. There was no life-altering event. The angels came in through the back door in a very gentle yet powerful way.

At the time, I was working in the biotech and pharmaceutical area doing clinical drug studies. I am a very practical, logical and commonsensical person. I first thought that I would retire in research, since that is what I had been doing for more than eight years. However, I guess I had a much different soul contract from what I was aware of consciously.

Yes, since I was little, I knew I was here to do something that would create a difference for humanity, and I clearly did not know how this was going to play out. Even so, by late fall of 2000, my life began changing.

My mother listens to the Howie Carr show (talk radio show in Boston, MA) almost every day. One day he had as his guest Doreen Virtue, a metaphysician and psychologist who communicates with the angelic realm. She was doing angel readings on the air and Mom, fascinated with what she was hearing, tried to call into the show to get an angel reading. "Sorry," she heard on the other end of the phone. All the lines were tied up and there was no more time left for calls. My Mom was very persistent, and Doreen's staff gave her a referral to another angel practitioner who had studied with her in California. This young man's name was Scott.

Eagerly Mom contacted Scott for an angel reading. After her reading, and for the first time in my life, I saw my Mom glow, and she kept bugging me to get an angel reading from Scott. Truthfully, I had no understanding at the time what an angel reading was. All I knew was that my Mom was very happy and glowing with peace.

About a month later, I phoned Scott. He was a soft-spoken young man and said, "Oh, I knew you were going to be calling me." I thought, 'Yeah buddy; tell me another one.' I was very skeptical, but I made an appointment anyway, for a week later.

Scott began our angel session by telling me about my angels. Then all of a sudden, he started talking to me about angels in general. It sounded like he was giving me an Angel 101 class. I listened intently and still was not sure what all of this meant. He told me during my time with him that I have two guardian angels and their names were Mary Elizabeth and George. I thought, 'George. Boy, that name does not sound too angelic.' Now I call him George of the Jungle. George has a great sense of humor.

Also, Scott advised that I read *Healing with the Angels*

by Doreen Virtue. At that time I did not know who Doreen Virtue was or even what she did. But Scott explained that she was the one with whom he trained and that this was an excellent book for beginners or for anyone who wanted to know more about angels.

I really did not want to write down the name of the book. But I thought if I did not, Scott would know psychically and I didn't want to get yelled at. So I followed his orders and wrote down the name of the book. The piece of paper that I wrote the name of the book on sat on my dining room table among all my other paperwork for about another month. It was two weeks before Christmas 2000 when I picked it up and said, "Oh, what do you know? That piece of paper is still here. I guess I need to check it out."

Because I was planning a quick trip to the mall to finish my holiday shopping, I took along the paper with the name of the book on it. Running into the Barnes and Noble bookstore to get some music and other little stocking stuffers, I decided to look up the angel book. There it was in the New Age section of the bookstore, only one copy left. On the cover was a picture of an angel holding a young child. It was beautiful! Then I looked at the price, which was very reasonable, and flipped through the book to see if I needed a Ph.D. or a theology degree to understand it, but it felt like an easy read. So I bought it!

Arriving home with many bundles, I started to sort out everything, among them the angel book. Taking the book out of the bag, I looked at it one more time and then literally tossed it on my kitchen table. The minute the book left my hand, I began hearing inside of my head, 'Pick up the book. Pick up the book tonight. Read the book tonight.'

The voice kept repeating itself over and over, until finally I said out loud in a very firm tone of voice, "Okay;

I will read the book tonight, but only after I put everything away, take my bath and get my pajamas on." Then the voice stopped, and I was able to finish putting away my holiday packages.

Sometimes I have an ADD (attention deficient disorder) moment and can easily get distracted. I took my warm relaxing bath and, coming out of the bathroom, I headed for bed completely forgetting about the book. I guess the angels knew that too! So once I started to walk into my bedroom to go to sleep, the voice started once again. "Don't forget the book. Read the book tonight. The book . . . the book." "Okay," I said. "I am getting the book right now." I picked it up and curled up in bed with it. Once I opened it and began to read it, I could not put it down. This simple book on angels touched me in a very miraculous way-- it ignited a spark of light in my soul.

Being a slow reader, I carried the book everywhere with me until I was done. I would read it in the morning while eating breakfast. I'd read it in the car while I was stuck in traffic, even during lunchtime at work and, of course, in the evening when I got home.

After fully consuming the book, I wanted more information on angels. I went back to the Barnes and Noble bookstore and got another angel book by the same author. With two books under my belt, I now needed to talk with someone about all this angel stuff and what it meant to me. I had questions and needed to process what I had read. But whom could I call? I dug out Scott's name and number and left him a message saying that I wanted another angel appointment. Scott was eager to hear what had happened and we set up another angel session.

While speaking with him on the phone, I told him about the book experience and then started asking some important questions that I had. About half an hour into our conversation, I said, "Scott, Doreen Virtue says that everyone can see their angels. I want to see my angels, but nothing happens and I don't see anything."

Scott said," Your angels are telling me that indeed they have been showing themselves to you." I responded, "No, they haven't. I don't see anything, Scott." Again he said, "Mary Elizabeth has been showing herself to you quite a bit." I started to argue with Scott, saying, "No, they haven't." The arguing back and forth went on for a little while and, at this point, I truly thought that Scott was making it up and that he was 'full of it.'

At the time I was in my bedroom with my phone headset on. I just happened to look over to the headboard of my bed while arguing with Scott, and I saw with my physical eyes a flash of light. I asked Scott if their energy could appear as a flash of white light. "Yes," he screamed, and those are called "angel lights," which is the energy of your angels that you can see with your eyes either open or closed. Oh God; I felt really terrible and embarrassed. I had been a "doubting Thomas' and thought that he was just making things up.

"Okay, Scott; yes you and my angels are right. I have been seeing them for quite some time now."

For a long time (maybe two years) I had been seeing these big sparks of light in my room at night. I was never afraid. In fact, I used to think that maybe I had something wrong with my eyes, and had even gone to the eye doctor, yet everything checked out fine. Then I thought maybe I was doing too much computer work or that I had something neurological going on. And yes, at one point the sparks were so big and bright, I thought that I had an alien visiting, taking pictures of my bedroom. Still not frightened by any of this, I would even say, "If you want to flash, just flash, because I am too tired and I am going to sleep. Happy flashing."

We both had a good laugh. Thank goodness Scott was patient and understanding. From that point on, we worked together on the phone once a month for spiritual mentoring sessions. He was my 'kick in the butt angel,' helping me to get on my path.

A few more weeks passed, and I went back to the Barnes and Noble bookstore, ready to read and learn more. I came across this small box of angel cards and thought it was an angel game. What did I know? Anyway, I got one more book, and I bought these angel cards and could not wait to get home to play with the new angel game.

Once home I quickly opened this box of angel cards and found out that it was not an angel game. They were angel oracle cards with messages from the angels. Now I was even more intrigued. Without even reading the little booklet that came with the cards, I started to shuffle and ask my angels a question. The cards were amazingly accurate. I asked if my guardian angels were with me. The first card that stuck out of the deck was--yes, you guessed it-- the "Guardian Angel" card. Wow, how cool was that! So I stayed up very late talking to my angels using these cards. I did not feel so alone anymore.

Chapter 7

ANGEL CAMP

F OR ALMOST SIX MONTHS Scott and I worked
together, discussing feelings, readings and theories. I
consumed book after book. I was like a sponge drinking up
all the information I could about angels. Then I ventured
out further, checking out Doreen Virtue's website. I was not
sure what I was looking for, but noticed that she offered an
Angel Therapy Practitioner TM (ATP) program. Admittedly,
I was excited yet at the same time had mixed feelings
because I was only familiar with her through her books.
I knew Scott trained with her but did not know of anyone
else. Still, that program remained in my thoughts.

The next time I was to have an angel mentoring session with Scott, I figured I would pick his brain about the
ATP program to see if it would be right for me. We talked
at length and he had loved his training. Knowing myself
to be very left brained (analytical and logical), I wondered
if "Angel Camp" was the next step. Scott was honest and
forthcoming with information about the program and then
he asked if I was going to take it. I responded that I honestly

didn't know right then. I was thinking that a person had to be very gifted to work with angels. What did I know? It was also a very expensive program.

About a month passed by and, off and on, I would think about angel camp. Still not sure what to do, I asked God and my angels. I told them that if they wanted me to go to angel camp to learn more and do this type of work, they were going to have to find the money for me, because I did not want to take it out of my bank account. I made a commitment to go provided they find the financial means of me going. Within one month of the start of the training program, I got an unexpected company bonus that paid for the whole trip. Amazing!!!! I felt truly blessed.

I had been working long hours at the biotech company and felt that I could really use a vacation. I arranged for vacation time, registered for angel camp and made my reservations for this angelic trip. Now this vacation was going to be a working vacation but, nonetheless, I was looking forward to going. I was not sure what to expect, but I knew I needed to be there.

I was a bit scared about traveling alone and being at this program for a full six days with all kinds of strangers. This was not my style at all, but I trusted and stayed positive and my deep spiritual journey was about to begin.

I was sitting in a classroom of about 125 people, and all were strangers to me. As the excitement was building in the room, Doreen came on stage. In a very soft and angelic voice, she began speaking to the group. I no longer remember what she was saying but something was being triggered within my heart. I sat in the middle of all these people and I felt something stir within me. I wanted to cry, and I couldn't hold the tears back. Here I was, sitting in this huge conference room, a sea of strangers all around me, and tears were pouring down my face. I had no idea what was happening, and all I wanted to do was run! Run as fast and as hard as I could--right back home.

My logical mind was on overload. I tried to think about what she was saying, and truly there was nothing that earth shattering. I simply could not understand why I was reacting that way as I struggled and fought with myself. A part of me wanted to stay, and yet another part of me wanted to run. I managed to stay in control until lunchtime, and then I had to leave the group. Everyone else ate together but I ran to my hotel room. I paced up and down, not knowing what to do. My heart was opened and now all of these feelings were just pouring out. I was losing control 'big time'.

With not even one friend in sight, I had no one to talk to and felt all alone. I thought quickly about what I would do and then it hit me. I needed to call Scott, my angel mentor, and maybe he could help me out.

I dug out his phone number and called. His phone just rang and rang, and only his answering machine came on. Breathlessly I said, "Scott, it's Elizabeth and I am here taking the ATP program with Doreen Virtue. I am feeling out of control and crying all over the place and don't even know why. I need help now and I feel like running and getting on the next plane back to New Hampshire."

I waited patiently for five minutes, then started pacing even more as I looked at the clock. Lunchtime would be over shortly and I needed to talk to someone. "Angels," I said, "I need to talk to Scott now and I feel like running. I don't understand what is happening, so please help me." I tried Scott again but had no luck in reaching him. I waited a couple more minutes and then tried one last time. He picked up.

"Hi, Elizabeth," he said with a warm reassuring voice.

"Scott, I have been trying to call you! I am in crisis here at Doreen's workshop." Scott responded by saying, "I happened to be on a call when the angels interrupted me and told me that I needed to take this call right away."

I replied, "Oh, thank you Scott. I really need to talk with you." I explained to him everything that was happening and what I was feeling. I still was crying as I spoke, so it was difficult at first to hear everything he was saying.

We talked for quite some time as he calmed me down and helped me to refocus. Scott was very understanding and explained to me that the energies of this experience were awakening and speaking to my soul. It was a profound awakening at the very core of my being and my Divine essence.

Composing myself, I returned to class, deeply grateful to Scott for taking the time to speak with me. He and the angels had responded to my SOS for help.

Over the next few days, I met many new friends and enjoyed myself. However, I had a run-in with my ego. Did you ever do that? I tell you, it's interesting. Many other students around me were seeing full body angels, getting tons of personal messages and having wonderful visions. What was I getting? Nothing! That's right; absolutely nothing. Well, maybe a few little things, but nothing like everyone else was getting. I felt stupid and like 'dummy the dunce.' I wondered to myself, 'God what was I thinking? I must have been crazy thinking that I could do this work.' I started believing that I had nothing to offer and that I must have made a mistake in taking this program. WHAT was I thinking?

I tried to remain positive while at the workshop, studied hard and wrote as fast as I could, taking down all kinds of notes on angels and angel healing techniques. I prayed and worked on opening myself up more psychically. This was all so very new to me, and I had no friends back home who were open to this or could even help me.

One of my new friends was Allison from Texas. She was a very special person. If nothing else, it was our time to meet. We had met for the first time at lunch one day. Lunchtime was crazy. I eat mostly meat and probably a lot of the wrong things, and I was trying to eat vegan during the course as recommended (teacher believed that eating vegan helps to raise your vibration so you can connect with the angels better). I call it all 'rabbit food' (no offense to the vegetarians and vegans). It's just not for me or at least not then.

Getting to lunch a little late that day, I filled my plate with mostly salad and bread and then began to look around for a seat. There were no vacant seats left next to anyone I'd already met, so I found myself sitting wherever I could. One of my new tablemates asked my name, I said, "Elizabeth." "Oh, you must be the Elizabeth that I need to connect with," she said. I thought that a little strange, but said with a smile, "Okay!" How could I have known that would be the beginning of a wonderful spiritual friendship that still continues today?

Allison's energy is quite different, and she reminds me of the Blessed Mother. She has helped me to stay grounded and focused on my spiritual work, acted as a good sounding board when I needed one and has helped me to stay within integrity. Allison has watched me through all of my growing pains and trials and tribulations and I am truly blessed to have her friendship as a part of my life and journey. She knows what unconditional love is, practices it, and has been a very strong spiritual mentor on my path.

On the last night of the program, I walked alone on the

sands of the beach, just gazing out over the ocean. It was the most beautiful night. The sky and all the stars and the moon were crystal clear. While just standing there on the beach and taking all of nature in--just for one moment--I saw with my own eyes off in the distance three beams of the whitest light I have ever experienced.

I was still sitting on the beach quietly enjoying the night when Allison found me and asked if she could sit with me. "Sure," I said, "I'd love to have your company." Others who had also been wandering along the shore seemed drawn to joining us, and before long, there must have been about 15 of us on the beach just relaxing, talking and hugging each other. It was the perfect night and the most perfect ending of my angel camp experience.

I returned home feeling a little sad because being with all these spiritual people was so nurturing and uplifting, I now felt empty and hated to leave it behind. What a difference from the first day when all I wanted to do was to go home!

For weeks I felt very alone, yet all too soon, I was once again entrenched in the daily grind of clinical research and the so-called real world. It was at this point that the real work of my journey began!

Chapter 8

MY JOURNEY BEGINS

ERE I WAS, JUST graduated from Angel Camp, and now what? I started thinking about what I could do. I certainly loved my angel experience and working with them, but what could I do and what could I offer? I truly had no clue!

I thought about creating a spiritual name for my new business. I had completed my Reiki training in 2001 and I wanted a business name that would bring in the essence of the angels as well as the healing energy of Reiki. I intuitively heard the angels giving me the name of "Divine Healing," which was perfect. Divine for God and the angels and Healing for the Reiki.

However, once I got my business name registered, I didn't know what to do next. I remember waking up early one Saturday morning contemplating my research job, dreading the thought of going back to work on Monday. My job seemed to be literally draining the life out of me. I began to cry and, feeling very hopeless, went into my bathroom and closed the door. It was totally dark in there and, while looking at the mirror in front of me, I could see the sparks and flashes of white light. I knew that these were my angels, and they were right there by my side.

I decided to ask my angels for some guidance. Crying and clearing away my tears, I sincerely asked my angels if I needed to look for another research job. I heard a soft "no." I asked again just to be certain of what I was hearing, and again I heard "no."

Still not totally trusting, I came out of the bathroom with bloodshot red eyes and tears streaming down my face, grabbed my angel cards and did a quick reading. I asked the same question again and drew three cards. The cards were confusing, and I could have interpreted them two different ways. Remember, I was still very new to all of this. The three cards drawn were printed with the notations "Truth and Integrity," "New Location" and "New Opportunity."

Baffled by these cards, I started to focus more on the New Location and New Opportunity. I thought at first that my angels were telling me to look for another research job, but then they brought my focus to the Truth and Integrity card. Research did not resonate with me any more. It did not speak to my truth and did not align with my personal integrity.

Standing with hands on my hips in the middle of my living room, I spoke to my angels and said, "Angels, I think you're telling me not to look for another research job but to stay focused on my Divine Healing practice. If this is the message that you are giving me, I want a clear, concrete sign today!" I stood waiting in my living room for a sign. Would Archangel Michael come in, or would I see lights in my home or would a feather or penny just show up, I wondered. I had all of these thoughts racing through my head, and truly needed some clear and concrete validation, but I wasn't sure how that was going to manifest itself to me.

It was early in the morning, about 8 am and I was very hungry, I'd forgotten to go to the grocery store for breakfast food. I think I gave the angels three minutes to respond to my request before heading for a McDonalds' breakfast. Nothing happened, so I got dressed and made my way to the McDonalds'.

The road was busy, but when I reached the parking lot, there were only a few cars. I thought that this was quite odd--but also that it was great. Fewer people meant faster service, and I could eat and run. With the scent of food in the air my ADD kicked in, and I was fully engaged in the breakfast experience completely forgetting about my request for a sign and validation from the angels.

So I ordered my "healthy" breakfast of pancakes, sausage, hash browns and coffee. After my food arrived, I turned around to see where I could sit. There were only about four to five people sitting on the right side of the room. The left side was completely empty, and that is where I wanted to sit, preferring my own space and privacy.

As I got settled and began to enjoy my breakfast, something caught my eye and drew my attention. I watched an elderly gentleman come through the door and go to the counter to order. I had never seen him before, but for some reason I kept one eye on him and the other on my breakfast.

He seemed very pleasant and was talking up a storm with the girls behind the register. He got his coffee, then did the same thing I'd done. He turned and scanned around to find where he wanted to go and started heading in my direction. As I sat there telepathically attempting to tell that man to go and sit somewhere else. What happened next was unbelievable!

This stranger, who I swear looked like a leprechaun, stopped right in front of my table, looked right at me and asked if I was feeling better! I quickly thought, 'Wow, this is really weird.' I responded, "Yes, my breakfast was good and I am feeling better." I was thinking, 'Okay, buddy. Keep moving. I want to be by myself.'

Instead of sitting elsewhere, this man decided to sit right beside me, and we talked for almost an hour about life, love, family and business. He talked about how at four different points in his life, he had started his own business. There was my sign, and I had almost missed it! Boy, the angels must have thought, 'This one is really dense.'

As he talked about business, I got the idea to pick his brain for some business advice. I asked him if I could ask him a question. He said, "Sure, you can ask me anything." So I told him that I was thinking about starting a new business. He stopped me and asked, "How old are you?" I said that I was 44. The number 4 in general is a very powerful number, according to the angels. When you see 4 or 44 or 444, it means that the angels are around you and encouraging and supporting you. Anyway, he said, "Forty-four is an excellent age to start a new business. What are you waiting for?"

"Wow," I thought. 'That is incredible.' He never asked me what kind of business I was thinking about or even if I had enough capital to get going. He spoke to me the whole time in a way that a father would speak to his child--very warm, loving, supportive and encouraging. I got my clear and concrete validation that instant but did not fully realize it until I got home and processed it a little more.

It was at this point that I truly started taking the angel work forward. I began to do readings on friends and colleagues. Even then I did not really know where all this would go. I was just having fun and exploring. My journey was just beginning. 'And yes, angels do hang out at McDonald's.'

Chapter 9

HEAVEN'S GIFT

I DID NOT COME FROM a strong line of metaphysicians nor had I had people in my own family who were openly psychic. Therefore, I never knew and no one ever told me that I had psychic potential and gifts. I was ignorant about the matter of psychic gifts and truly thought and believed that only "special" people were gifted with intuition. Oh boy, was I wrong. Everyone has psychic potential and there is no exception. The gift of intuition is our God given gift or heaven's gift to humanity. Our psychic gifts are how God, the angelic realm and the spirit world speak to us.

After attending angel camp, I slowly began discovering my gifts and potential. How cool is that to be able to offer to do a psychic reading on someone? I think it's awesome!

I started to read more about psychic development and even took a psychic development workshop with John Holland, who is an internationally known psychic and medium located here in New Hampshire. John made learning fun and helped me to understand more of my own gifts. Angel camp was great, but this psychic development class with John gave me a firmer footing through an understanding of my own intuitive gifts.

When I do an angel reading, it is a combination of using angel oracle cards along with my intuition to get additional information and messages from the angels. Historically, it's been very hard for me to trust. For most of my life I had been told repeatedly that I was not smart or talented enough. So I kept practicing and trying to trust each time, trying every time to get validation. My angels kept telling me to trust. I thought, 'Oh boy, how could I trust so completely and deeply when I am just awakening to my gifts? It seems like my angels have more faith in me than I have in myself." So I told my angels that I needed more validation for just a little while longer. When extra faith in oneself and validation is requested, it is never denied.

I had wonderful opportunities to practice on some friends and especially on people at work. Once word got out at work that I went to angel camp and that I was doing angel readings, people started lining up for appointments. They started asking me for readings. I felt honored, and, because I was still working on trust and doing readings, I did all readings for free because I still was not completely sure of myself.

This all changed one summer day in 2001. It was mid-July and I was employed at a biotechnology company in Massachusetts. Word of my angel readings made it to Doreen, the Director of Human Resources. She called me into her office and confronted me about the readings. I gulped and said, "Yes, I do angel readings," and, in a defensive tone, continued on to add that I did them after working hours. She said that she had heard wonderful things about them and was now curious. She asked if I was willing to do a reading on her after work. Although I was scared out of my mind, something inside made me say, "Sure." So we set up an angel appointment even though I was feeling very anxious about the whole thing. I started thinking, 'What if I can't get anything? What will she think of me? What if I mess up?' My ego was in full gear and having a field day. I counted each day as they went by, and then finally the day came for Doreen's angel reading.

It was late on Friday afternoon. Just about everyone had gone home except for the CEO and CFO. Nervous that I would be found out at this top level of management, I was really trying to trust my angels, even though I still had some doubts.

As we started with her reading, I told her about the angels that were around her and gave her their names. She listened intently, for her angels had much to say regarding her love life, and her son and her finances.

Everything seemed to be going very smoothly until her last question. Now Doreen had been with the company for only about six months, and she seemed pretty happy with her job. However, her last question was, "Will this company allow me to do what I really want to do?" That was her question. She did not elaborate on what her true deepest passion was for work. I began talking to my angelic team and started pulling some angel cards. The cards that I was getting were not making any sense. I wasn't getting anything, and I was struggling to make sense of what was being presented to me. Knowing I was in trouble, Doreen started to look at the cards to see if she could make some sense out of them. Nothing was coming together, and I thought, 'Great; I must look like a real fool.'

After a few minutes (which seemed like hours) went by, I heard them tell me that she would be leaving the company soon. This was a little soft voice in my head that I was hearing. My angels were moving me away from the cards, and I was doing a straight intuitive reading. I just went with the flow and spoke. I told her that the angels were talking to me and that the cards were not necessary right now.

Doreen said, with panic in her voice, "What do you mean? I just got here and I am very happy! I don't understand!" She said that she was not looking for another job and that she was happy with her newly found home at the biotech company.

"Okay," she finally said, "Where exactly am I going?" I asked the angels, and they showed me a white building with some red lettering. I could not make out the letters, but I could see her standing on the second floor in the middle of a walkway. She stood tall and was dressed all in black, wearing gold jewelry and holding a briefcase, with a smile on her face that went from ear to ear. Her angels whispered to me that she would be doing her heart's passion and that it would be big money. I relayed this information and also explained what I was seeing. I told her that this new position did not feel like a human resources position, which was the area that she had worked in for most of her life. Her career change felt like it was something brand new. "But Elizabeth," she said, "I am not looking for a new job. I don't understand."

"Okay. When exactly am I going to be making this move?" she asked. I asked her angels for additional information, and they led me back to where she was standing on that walkway. There were several windows on both sides of her. The sun was out and leaves were still on the trees. I got the impression that it was summer or maybe early fall. Then the angels showed me the number eight. I was not sure what the eight meant. I explained everything that I was getting and shared with her the number eight. "What does that mean, Elizabeth?" she asked. I replied that the eight could mean in eight days, eight weeks, eight months from now or the eighth month, which would be August, and we were already in mid-July. It could also mean eight years from then, but I felt like it was right around the corner.

Still not truly sure what was happening, Doreen said, "It can't be in eight days, for I am not even looking for a job at this point. The eighth month doesn't make sense either, because it's too soon. I am not sure if I buy this, Elizabeth."

This was supposed to be my first paid reading, but because of what she just said and not fully trusting what I was getting, I just let the whole reading go for free. I felt really bad about my performance and even felt like an idiot.

August came quickly and, close to the end of August, Doreen pulled me into her office and said, "Shut the door." There was so much political stuff going on at work, I did not know if I was getting fired, laid off or if the company was closing all together. I held my breath and walked into her office. "Shut the door," she said, "Just shut the door. Now I was really nervous.

"Sit Elizabeth...sit," she said, pointing to the chair in front of her desk. I sat quietly and just listened.

She asked me if I remembered her angel reading back last month. I nodded my head, indicating that yes, I did. "Well," she said. "You'll never guess what just happened." She talked for quite some time and explained that before she came to this company, she had sent her resume out to several different companies. At the end of July, she had decided to work from home one day. While at home, a major office supply company had phoned her and said that they had had her resume on file for the past year and they had just created a brand new position and thought she would be perfect for it and a nice addition to their team.

Doreen was very animated as she spoke of her conversation with this company. She said that she kept telling them that she was very happy at the biotech company for which she was now employed, but they kept insisting on at least having her come in for an interview. Doreen continued to resist, firmly stating that she was very happy and was not interested in making any career move right then. The Human Resource person on the phone finally asked Doreen how much money it would take for her to make a career move. Doreen responded naming a large figure for her salary, which she thought they would consider too outrageous and drop everything.

They did not, and she finally agreed to an interview. The position, Director of Associate Relations and Diversity, suited Doreen perfectly. This was an upper management position and the amount of money that she'd told them was the amount to which they agreed. Not only did all of this change transpire in August, the eighth month, but the company was also only eight minutes from home. Doreen then paid me for her reading and thanked me deeply.

Chapter 10

REIKI AND THE DIVINE

I'D NEVER INTENDED TO learn Reiki or become a Reiki Master/Teacher. I did have Reiki sessions for my own health but always thought that you had to be a very special person with great connections to do Reiki. What was I thinking?

All the same, my Reiki teacher who worked on me said that she was going to give me my Reiki attunement so that I could work on myself in case I could not get to her.

My introduction to Reiki came after I had been diagnosed with sarcoidosis, which is an autoimmune disorder that can affect the major organs in the body (heart, lungs, liver, etc.) and the only drugs that are used for this debilitating disease are steroids. In general, steroids are wonderful drugs that do exactly what they are intended to do, but there are several serious side effects especially with long-term usage. The only choices I had were to take steroids or be hooked up to an oxygen tank.

Neither of these therapies was appealing, but I decided to take the steroids and did for several years just to be able to breathe. My lungs, eyes and liver were severely affected by the sarcoidosis. I had almost lost my vision all together and, because it was also in my lungs, I had a very difficult time breathing. Just making my bed each morning would take about 20 minutes because I would get so tired. Getting dressed to go to work was another big tiring ordeal. My lungs are still affected today with scar tissue, so running a marathon is not in my near future.

At that time, I was working for a medical device research organization. As a result of the disease, I would cough and cough, driving everyone around me crazy including myself. I used to even pound on my chest because of the anger. I could not understand why my lungs were not healing and I resented taking the medication.

This is why eventually I decided on my own to cut back on the steroids and try to manage the condition from an alternative medical point of view. I tried various vitamins and different vitamin concoctions. But nothing alleviated my constant coughing and short breath.

Finally the people physically around me at work were getting tired and annoyed at my coughing throughout the day. One gal came up to me and handed me a piece of paper with the word Reiki on it with a person's name and phone number. I inquired as to what Reiki was and why she was giving me this information. She replied, "We are tired of hearing you cough and you better make an appointment. It may help you and if you don't we'll take you out back and string you up by your toes." Just call and make the appointment, she said.

I was rather self-conscious of my coughing and knowing that I had tried everything to keep it quiet with no success, I made that phone call.

The Reiki experience was great but I did go through a

severe healing crisis. After the third Reiki session in mid-September 2000, the weather was perfect and while driving home with all of the car windows open, I started feeling cold. I rolled the windows up halfway and thought that I should be just fine. However, the cold feeling continued even after I closed all of the windows. I then put a little heat on in the car which was a crazy thing to do since it was a beautiful fall evening and about 70 degrees outside. After all this, I was still cold so I cranked up the heat in the car all the way.

I arrived home about an hour later and when I stopped the car and shut off the heat, the coldness came right back and I began to shiver uncontrollably. It was late Friday night around 11:30 pm and not a soul was in sight. I dragged myself out of the car and began my climb up three flights of stairs. I was totally exhausted and out of breath, but made it up the stairs slowly by literally crawling on all fours. By the time I made it to my apartment and opened my door, I knew something serious was up. I decided to take my temperature, which read 104-degrees and was extremely high for me since my normal temperature runs around 96.9 degrees.

I threw myself in the shower and just ran the hot water. My fingers were turning white and I kept shivering. It was late, I was all alone and did not know what to do. I could have gone to the emergency room, but what could they do? I was sure my regular doctor was away. So I just finished my shower, got ready for bed and piled blankets on top of me. I burrowed deep into my blankets and finally fell asleep.

I did sleep all through the night, but by morning I was still running a high fever and felt achy all over. I took some fever medicine, but my fever only dropped by a couple of degrees. I ate light and drank as much as I could. By 10:30 pm that day, all of my symptoms magically disappeared. They left just as quickly as they appeared.

I continued receiving Reiki until my teacher thought it would be a good idea to attune me to Reiki II. This made me a healing practitioner though I still did not know it was going to become part of my career.

The Reiki energy helped to open more of my third eye which is the doorway to clairvoyance (which means clear seeing) and is one of your psychic gifts. It was at this time I began seeing flashes of white light with my physical eyes. Those are the angels that I spoke earlier about. I started to see those lights every night even though at the time I did not know what they were.

My Reiki practice began to flourish and then I started teaching Reiki. At first I only offered to teach the Master/ Teacher level because there were so many people teaching levels I and II. But then some of my angel students began asking me to teach level II.

Some then asked if I offer level I Reiki workshops. So I now teach all the levels of Reiki and I have had some pretty incredible experiences with teaching as well as during private healing sessions.

Regardless whether I am conducting a class or doing an angel reading or even a healing session, I truly never know what is going to happen, believing simply that it is always in perfect and Divine order and that person receives whatever they need.

I always begin my healing sessions with prayer, intention and then invite my whole spiritual team, which includes my angels, higher self, guides, ascended masters that work with me like Jesus, Master Buddha, the Divine Mother or Mother Mary, Saint Germain of the violet flame and many of the Archangels. I work closely with Archangel Michael for clearing and protection. Next, I call forth Archangels Raphael for healing and to assist in guiding the healing energies, and Metatron to help balance out the frequencies of light and adjust the energy vibration of my client as well as myself. Archangels Ariel and Gabriel are always close behind to assist with psychological trauma and to help me be clear about the information that I am getting.

I remember once having a young man come to me for a Reiki session and after working on him with chakra tuning forks and anointing him with Spikenard oil (Spikenard oil is sacred oil that supposedly Mary Magdalene used to anoint Christ's feet), I began to work on his crown chakra (head area). Just then, Christ showed up at the foot of the Reiki table, looked at me and said, "Thank you for taking care of my flock." I shared this experience with the young man and we both felt very blessed.

Another time, one of my angel students, Brenda, came to me for a Reiki session and as always, I invited Christ to be there and to help out. Well this was going to be a very unique experience for Brenda.

We talked at first about Reiki in general and then proceeded with the session. Everything was proceeding normally when suddenly I noticed her shaking and trembling. First I thought that may be it was too much energy and I intuitively asked my team if I needed to back away for a little bit. They all said "no." I asked Brenda if she was alright and all she said was "He's here." I knew what she meant and asked again if she was okay. "Yes, but he's here, isn't he Elizabeth?" I said, "Oh do you mean Christ?" "Yes," Brenda replied. I laughed and explained to her that I invited him here to assist me with her Reiki session. "Oh but Elizabeth, he is really here." "Yes, Brenda he is." Brenda has been struggling with worthiness issues for most of her life and she could not understand why Christ would show up for her. I let her know that she is a Master as well and that her soul mission here is to remember her connection to the Divine and to begin to recognize herself as the Master that she truly is.

Some deceased loved ones came in and just held her hands while I finished her session. Today, Brenda is in the process of developing her own healing practice in Maine.

I continue to hold gratitude in my heart and soul and am grateful for the profound effects of Divine love in the form of Reiki, in my own life and the lives of so many I meet.

Chapter 11

MY SPIRITUAL CONTRACT

I WAS STILL WORKING IN clinical research and, one night a week, I would coordinate a Reiki clinic for a local healing center. I enjoyed and loved my Thursday nights there, thinking that I would stay in clinical research and just work a little angel stuff on the side. Then I thought that maybe I could combine the Reiki and the angel stuff together. So I did some research on my own and found that I could do an angel healing circle, which brought in the love and energy of the angels along with the Reiki energies to help release blockages, fears, anxieties and unforgiveness. This was a great idea, I thought, and now I needed to get my idea approved.

Being so enthusiastic and passionate about this new idea, I decided to speak with the director of the healing center, who also thought that this was a great idea. But then she said, "Elizabeth no one knows anything about angels, so you will need to teach at least one class on angels, and then we can offer the angel healing circle." 'Rats," I thought. 'How did this happen? I don't want to teach. God, I get so

59

nervous speaking in public. Now I have to teach. No way,' I said. I tried two other healing centers, and they all said the same thing. Teach at least one class on angels, and then we can offer the angel healing circle. I thought, 'What is going on here?' I was feeling very defeated and discouraged. I was ready to throw in the towel and just say forget it and continue on my regular path of research and doing the Reiki clinic.

My soul was restless and kept nudging me to try this. So I told God and the angels that I would give teaching a try. My first three classes that I taught in the late fall were awful! I judged myself, determined that teaching was not my thing, that I was a lousy teacher and pulled myself out of the teaching arena. But my soul still felt uneasy and restless!

One month passed and it was now January of 2002. My soul kept encouraging me to try teaching again. I argued back and forth with myself. Once I made up my mind--that was all that it took to get the ball rolling. This time I made a commitment to God and angels that I would be the spiritual teacher and healer that I was meant to be. I told them that if this were truly my path and spiritual contract, they would need to teach me how to teach, where to teach, and what to teach, and they would need to teach me about business, as well. I was not fortunate enough to have an available spiritual teacher or mentor who could help me. Talk about a tall order! But that was what I told them.

I was willing to do the work, and I needed their help and guidance to make it happen. They did just that! I found out very quickly how NOT to teach, and now I needed to learn how to teach effectively and to make it fun.

I decided to move forward and asked God, Archangel Michael, Archangel Gabriel and my guardian angels to help me with the spiritual business and to be my business partners. They quickly accepted my offer. Archangel Gabriel, whose energy is bright copper-colored gold, showed up and followed me around my home that day. Huge flashes of gold-colored light kept showing up right behind me everywhere I went.

The angels guided me to contact certain places to teach and, at first, had me focus on just a couple of classes. This was to get my feet wet and to help me to start feeling comfortable.

I felt truly blessed by all of this. I had no one to open any doors or who could spiritually lead me down that path that I was now on. It was all a matter of faith and an open willingness to come out of my spiritual closet. This was a big turning point on my spiritual path, and angels guided me all the way.

My spiritual contract as a Lightworker is to help to awaken souls to their divinity, assist them with creating their connection to the Divine so they can begin to recognize themselves as the Master they truly already are.

Chapter 12

ARCHANGEL MICHAEL

ARCHANGEL MICHAEL IS A mighty powerful arch-angel and helps me to remember who I am and to stay focused on my spiritual path. Michael carries a blue, flaming sword of love. Those who are clairvoyant can see his sword. I have. It's very cool and can be used to clear away negativity and sever any energetic cords (energy draining cords).

Archangel Michael's energy is very particular. I always know when he is around. He has a very large and very loving presence. Michael is my closest and best friend and has helped me out of several difficult situations.

One time, I decided to just take a mini get-away from the office. It was in March and still very bitterly cold. I packed up my snowshoes thinking to get a little exercise and drove to a closed down ski resort.

While driving into the parking lot, I had the gut feeling to turn around immediately. Did I listen? Of course not! I was determined to go snow-shoeing no matter what. At this point, I could begin to feel ice underneath me and then it happened.

My wheels started spinning and I got stuck. I could have kicked myself in the butt for not listening to my feeling but I knew that the angels would help me.

So I started asking the angels for some help. I did what I could to get my vehicle free, but nothing worked. I tried putting paper under my tires and even some window washer fluid thinking that may be it would melt some of the ice. But this only made matters worse.

Still calling on the angels, I then thought that I could try to flag someone down on the main road and see if someone would help me.

The cars drove by very fast, and being out there flagging someone down made me even more uncomfortable. So I walked back to my vehicle. Feeling very disgusted and let down I began screaming at the angels for some help. I had been asking very nicely but nothing was happening. So I said, "Archangel Michael get your butt down here right now and get me unstuck. I have done everything that I could humanly do and I am tired, cold and it's starting to snow again and I have to go to the bathroom. So get down here right now and get me out of this mess and thank you!"

Well the heavens must have panicked with me screaming down here. I got back into my vehicle and low and behold, I was out in less than 30 seconds. I did say thank you to everyone and then made my journey back home. So much for my exercise out in nature.

I once had a reading with Ronna Herman, she is a wonderful lady who channels Archangel Michael. Here is what Michael had to say:

ARCHANGEL MICHAEL

"Dear Beloved One: You are making great strides as you progress along the path of initiation, and it is now time for you to remember your heritage. You are of angelic lineage; you carry the Essence of angels within your DNA and heart/soul. You are one of our beloved own. Most often, we do not give this information until we feel you are ready to acknowledge the vastness of who you truly are.

You have traveled with me and Archangel Faith, who carries the Goddess aspects of the First Ray of Divine Will and Power, throughout the eons of time and we have had many wondrous adventures together. Your journey on Earth has been long and arduous and you have suffered much on your spiritual mission. You have had many important lifetimes where you had great responsibilities, and also many simple ones where your main objective was to seek solitude, enjoy nature and attune to the Earth and the animal kingdom. Regardless of your situation in life, we have always guided you via that small still voice within and during your dreams, and we have protected you when you were weak and discouraged. Even though you do not remember, you were never alone.

Dear one, you have stepped onto a narrow path where many fear to follow, but you have always been a brave and daring soul. The failures from the past have given you the wisdom and courage you need to fulfill this, your greatest mission on Earth. In many lifetimes, you have allowed your family or those you loved to divert you from your spiritual path. Know that you are not responsible for anyone's spiritual growth but your own. Fill yourself with the elixir of Love/ Light from the heart of the Creator and then allow that wondrous energy to flow forth from your heart center. Be the example, be the wayshower, display your self-mastery and allow the miracles that you deserve to manifest in your life. In that way, you will best serve those around you.

You, as many others, are in the midst of an accelerated transformational process, whereby you are continually processing energy that no longer serves you—core issues from deep within. Allow us to be your guide and follow that small voice within which is our way of communicating with you at the present. As you awaken to your God-consciousness and the magnificence of who you are, it is your own private journey and no one else can tell you how to proceed. Do not fear change, beloved, allow those things that no longer serve you to melt away. Step through the fear and see it melt away, leaving a bright new future before you. Know that we are ever near to guide and protect you—we are only a heartbeat and a thought away.

It is time for you to reclaim your birthright. REMEMBER, you agreed to be a part of the great experiment on planet Earth, and you promised to be our representative on the physical plane so that we could radiate our love and energy to humanity. Before you embodied that first time, we gave you a symbolic sword—the sword of Divine will, truth, and valor. Use that sword to sever any discordant energies that are keeping you shackled to the illusion of the third dimension—claim your symbolic wings, beloved, and come, soar with us. Accept the gift of Divine will and power we offer you as you strive to reclaim your mastery. Allow the love we feel for you to radiate forth from your heart center to those just awakening.

And also remember, dear one, LOVE IS THE FUEL OF ANGELIC BEINGS. Know that you are loved and protected. Call on us, we will answer." I AM ARCHANGEL MICHAEL

Chapter 13

A TEST AND A LEAP OF FAITH

EVERY PSYCHIC THAT I had seen told me that I would stay in clinical research and move up the corporate ladder. How far from the truth! No one foresaw how I was going to transform "down the road." In truth, it's just as well, because if they had seen that and they had told me, I probably would have run in the opposite direction.

There I was--still working in clinical research and working long, hard hours and thinking about the angel work. Slowly I had come out of my spiritual closet and started telling a few people about the angels and about the angel training. One by one, each person at work started to contact me for an angel reading, and then I began teaching a few classes in the evening. At first only two classes, but then things started to shift and change very quickly with the angel work.

While still working for a biotech company, I slowly built

my spiritual practice. I saw clients and conducted lectures and presentations in the evening and on the weekends. This did not leave me much time for myself.

I continued at this pace for some time, and then one day the vice president of this biotech company that I was working for in Watertown, Massachusetts called me into her office and said, "Foley, sit down. I need to talk to you." I, of course, sat down and gulped! What possibly could be happening that the VP needed to talk with me?

The VP was a woman who was extremely tough and judgmental, a perfectionist who smokes a cigar and tries to be "one of the boys." Power and control was her aim and everyone was intimidated by her--even the CEO of the company. I do give her credit because she was a very hard worker, extremely knowledgeable and always had a great story to tell. She had a wonderful laugh, but was not some-one you want to cross or get on her "bad side."

That morning, I sat quietly with my hands clasped together on my lap and waited. The VP said that they were eliminating my position altogether, but that they liked the work I did and wanted to somehow keep me employed. The company wanted to offer me a position of Clinical Trial Specialist, which meant that I would need to travel 65-85% of the time and go to various medical centers to validate data and the status of the clinical trial.

I began to panic and became paralyzed with fear. Deep down, I knew that my spiritual business was doing well, but I wasn't ready to take that leap of faith yet. I wasn't sure that I could financially support myself. While I worked my regular day job, which did support me well, I did not have to worry about making a lot of money with my spiritual work.

I experienced waves of joy, knowing that the job I really

hated was coming to a quick end, but then I began to have waves of panic and anger. 'What a mess,' I thought, and 'How was this going to work out?'

I listened to all that the VP said, and then I tried to explain that I had started my own company on the side and that my nights and weekends were already committed. I could not possibly accept this Clinical Trial Specialist position because of all the travel that was required.

The VP looked surprised and then asked what my business was about. 'Oh boy,' I thought, 'Now, how do I explain angels to someone who is a VP and a double Ph.D. degree person?' I decided to "come clean" and just spoke my truth about the spiritual business. I told her that I teach about angels throughout New England and see private clients, as well.

If looks could kill, I would have been dead on the spot. "What?" the VP replied. "Look, young lady. We pay you big bucks, and if I want to learn about angels and religion, I'll go to church. So get your priorities straight and make up your mind. I want your decision on my desk first thing Monday morning. Are we clear?"

Feeling very low and angry, I said in a very soft tone of voice, "Yes, we are clear."

I left the VP's office and headed right for the bathroom. In there I cried, verbalized my anger, and truly did not know what to do. After I composed myself, I went outside and sat in my car. I cried even more and then started screaming to my angels. I was so busy yelling at them that they had no room to respond!

I told God and the angels that I was not ready to make a complete career transition. I explained that I was very grateful for all the spiritual work and the abundance, but I was not confident enough to just "jump ship." I began to panic even more.

The weekend was coming and, instead of being joyful, I was in a complete state of turmoil. There was no one who could truly help me figure this one out. I needed to talk with my angels and get clarity on what to do.

Monday morning came, and I appeared at the VP's office, bright and early. I wasn't sure if I could go through with this, but it was time. I knocked on the VP's door, and she motioned for me to come in. She asked me if I had made a decision and I said, "Yes."

I explained to her that my spiritual work was extremely important to me and that I had already made teaching commitments. I was shaking in my shoes, but the words just came right out. It was to be a moment of truth for me.

As I spoke, I did tell her that I had enjoyed working for the company, and I thanked her for the opportunity to stay on. Then I asked if there was something else I could do to stay on at the company. She bluntly replied, "No," without any emotion, and she told me to wrap up my work and that Friday would be my last day of employment there.

I argued a little with her by saying that just having five days to wrap things up and try to find another job was not fair. I boldly asked if I could have until the end of the month, instead. She asked,

"Why should I give you a month?"

I said, "Because I am asking you to."

Incredibly, she agreed, and I quickly and quietly returned to my desk and started to clear things out. I wasn't sure why I was doing this now, but I took care of my clinical responsibilities and packed my things.

I tried to talk with the Director of Human Resources, but he would not help me. He, too, was afraid of the VP and feared the loss of his own position. It was clear that I had no one on my side and that no one would even go and fight for me. Not even my own boss, who was a very considerate person, would defend me because he feared for his own job, as well.

The day flew by quickly and, before I knew it, I was all packed and it was time to go home. At the time, I didn't realize that that would be my last day there. But on some intuitive level I had an inner knowing that I would not be returning. As it turned out, with my accumulated vacation and sick time I was able to receive my requested month's notice without having to return.

I asked the universe and the angels to help me find another research job right away. I also decided to use some of my personal time to contact recruiters and surf the web for other clinical trial positions. Within two weeks, I found another research job, but this one was different.

It was now April of 2002 and, after going on three interviews, I accepted a contract research position for a major pharmaceutical company in Cambridge, Massachusetts. The contract position started in May and would last six months, at the end of which, I could either go to a different job or stay on if the company wanted me. The contract position felt very freeing to me.

This company was great, and everyone seemed to help everyone. But now my spiritual practice was growing by leaps and bounds. I was only taking time to eat and sleep, and the rest of my time was spent working on the trials and teaching and doing angel readings.

Every day I was getting calls for readings and for classes. It was wild. At that time I was working three jobs. I had my research position, my own spiritual business on the side and I was doing readings for a metaphysical store in Arlington, Massachusetts. So you see, I was busy and staying out of trouble.

However, by mid-July, I was getting very tired of commuting every day by car and train to work. Fighting traffic was not my thing, and it did wear on me, despite listening to books on tape.

One Tuesday while driving to the train station, I mentally talked to God and my angels and told them, 'Thank you for all these wonderful opportunities to help me with the readings and the classes, but this schedule is just a bit too much.' I was getting overtired and cranky. My day would end around midnight, and then I would get up around 5:30 am to start my morning commute again. I was getting tired of the "rat race."

I told the angels that I did not think I could last until October, when my research contract would be completed, but that I wanted to somehow keep my promise to finish this project. I could not imagine how this was going to play out, and I asked for a clear, concrete sign if it was time for me to leave my research career and even retire from research and that I would be financially okay. Once you ask for a sign, you just need to let go and let God figure out the best way to validate a response to you.

So I finished my commute and began the day as usual. However, Tuesday afternoons were reserved for our clinical trial meeting. The purpose was to review data, problems and timelines. The clinical trial team gathered together as we did every Tuesday, but something was going to be different--in fact, highly irregular.

Our boss, Patty, decided to attend, and she spoke to us about the timelines for the project. She said that she had some good news and some bad news. Everyone said, "Tell us the bad news first." The bad news was that the timeline for completing this project was moved from October 31st to August 30th.

Wow; was this great news! I took this as my angelic sign that my time in clinical research was winding down, and I silently celebrated this new change. This meant that I only had to work one and a half more months and that I could still complete my project. God and the angels have a unique way to assist. I never saw this one coming. Not only did I have just about another month and a half, but I could also keep my promise to finish the project, which I truly wanted to do. This company and the people were all so very nice, and I did not want to disappoint them or burn any bridges behind me.

So I decided that on August 1st I would hand in my notice. I did not tell a soul that I was going to do this. I kept it a secret between the angels and me.

August 1st came and I became nervous about giving notice. I had a hard time pulling my thoughts together. The day ended, and I felt terrible because I did not give my notice. Something was stopping me, and it was my old fear again.

Even though I had received my sign and it was a perfect solution to my situation, I began again to worry about the money and being able to financially support myself. I called in sick the next day, just to have a little more time to process this new situation. I called on my friend, Archangel Michael, to help calm down my fears and to give me strength and courage to go and give my notice.

On August 3rd, I was busily at work reviewing clinical trial data when Patty suddenly popped into my office. I truly liked Patty. She was the most wonderful boss I had ever had. Patty was knowledgeable, respectful, understanding and had a great sense of humor. Well, before I knew it, words flew out of my mouth and I said, "Patty, do you have some time today to talk?" Oh my God, what did I just say? Am I crazy? Where did these words come from?

She said, "Sure, what about right now, and we can go in my office?" I gulped again and said, "Great!" So I followed upstairs to her office, and she closed the door and asked what was up. In retrospect, I could see history repeating itself, and I sure hoped that this talk would go a lot better than the one when I had worked for the biotech company.

"Patty," I started to say, "I know you probably don't know this, but I have my own private business on the side that I work at on evenings and weekends. My business has really grown in a way that I did not anticipate." I continued to explain to Patty that it was becoming too much for me and that I needed to give my notice.

Right away, she asked what I did for work. Again I was having flashbacks of what had happened before when I was asked this question. But the words just flowed out of my mouth--with love. I bravely and boldly told Patty about my angel business and the classes. First there was silence--and that silence seemed to last forever, but then Patty said, "This is different, but it sounds very cool."

She immediately asked if I could stay on until the project was complete. I told her that I was committed to doing so - I would work until the end to finish it. I shared with her my feelings about the company and said that the shift in timelines was actually a blessing in disguise for me. I told her about my conversation with the angels--about my schedule and that I had asked for a sign when she had told us last month about the change in the deadline date for finishing the project. I said that this was my sign that it was time to move on.

Our meeting ended on a positive note, and she even

inquired about my website and class schedule. I hugged Patty and thanked her for being understanding.

I finished the day on a positive note, but now I had to tell my family. Oh God; this was going to be a challenge. But I trusted my inner guidance and the guidance from the angels.

While on the way to teach that same evening, I called my mom on the cell phone and told her the news. She said, "What? Are you crazy? You're leaving that wonderful job and all that money?" I told her that the spiritual business had grown so much that now my full-time job was interfering with my spiritual business. I told her that I had spoken with my angelic team and asked for a sign that it was time for me to retire from research and that I would be financially all right. I went into details about everything because, up until that point, I had not shared any of my thoughts with her.

My mom went right into freak mode, and I wasn't going down that path with her. I stood in my own power, trusted what I was being guided to do, spoke my truth and then took the guided action of giving notice.

Mom panicked and phoned my brother in California, who then left me a message at home that went something like this. "Hi, there. Mom said that you quit your full-time job and plan to be doing just the angel work. I just want you to know that I give you a lot of credit and, if you need any money, just let me know and I will try to help out. Talk with you later. Bye, Rick."

I arrived home late that night, feeling exhausted from all the day's events: talking to my boss, giving notice, working my regular job and then teaching an angel class that night. When I got home, I picked up all of my messages, more people had called requesting private appointments for angel readings. I just had to laugh when I got to my brother's message. Bless his heart for wanting to help out.

I called Rick the next day to thank him for his generosity and assured him that I would be just fine. Everything was in Divine and perfect order, and failure was not an option.

The month ended perfectly! I finished my work on the project by August 31st and on Sept 1st 2002, I was working for God and the angels, full-time.

A few months passed, and my old boss Patty surprised me one day by scheduling an angel reading with me and then attending one of my angel classes. It was great to see her, and I gave her a huge hug. I thanked her a gazillion times for her understanding and support of my work. We still stay in touch, even to this day.

I took a leap of faith and never looked back. I trusted my spiritual helpers and myself, and I have no doubt that I did the right thing by leaving the corporate world. I now know that I am truly on my Divine path and being guided all the way.

Chapter 14

THE SPIRIT WORLD

I NEVER HAD THE DESIRE to do mediumship. For those who do not know what it is, mediumship means connecting and communicating with the spirit world to receive messages from deceased loved ones. Mediumship can bring great healing to someone who, in particular, is feeling depressed about losing a family member or a dear friend.

Some of the benefits of mediumship assist with healing from grief, guilt, sadness or other feelings of great loss, and it is a powerful way to prove that we do indeed survive death. We are eternal beings of light and love and can never die. Connecting with a deceased loved one can often help us to lose our fear of physical death.

I must honestly admit that I was scared out of my mind at the idea of doing mediumship. First I thought, 'Well, you must need to be a very special person to do this type of work.' Then when I went to Angel Camp, Dr. Virtue started to talk to us about this. She claimed that one could learn how to connect to the spirit world, and that the deceased people on the other side looked better than we do. I silently laughed and did not buy one word of what she was saying. The more I thought about doing mediumship, the more I got scared.

Dr. Virtue began her talk about mediumship, and I don't remember very much from her lecture about this topic because I just blocked it. One of her books has a chapter devoted to mediumship, and I read all the chapters except for that one. Then my private practice started taking off, and, for a period of about two weeks, I kept getting inquiries from people who wanted to connect with a deceased loved one. I kept telling them that mediumship was not my specialty and I would refer them.

After this two-week medium spree, I decided to have a heart-to-heart talk with my dear friend and angelic boss, Archangel Michael. I asked Michael, "Why are the angels sending me people who want mostly mediumship type of readings?" His response was, "You need to lose your fear around mediumship, and we can help you."

Oh, what a wake-up message that was. "All right," I said. "Then let's work together on this." I explained to my angels and Michael that I first did not know if I could do mediumship. Second, I told them that I was somewhat scared by the thought of seeing or connecting with a deceased loved one. You know Hollywood has done an excellent job of scaring the life out of me with all the horrid movies like "Night of the Living Dead" and other scary movies. I guess I thought that a deceased person would show up like they do in the movies. You know--headless, bloody and dismembered. I really did not know what to expect, but I expected the worst.

I diligently worked with Archangel Michael for one week, asking him each and every night to work with me while I was asleep to remove any fears, anxieties, blocks and obstacles to connecting with deceased loved ones and doing mediumship. Each morning I awoke feeling no different than the next day. I just had to trust that my angels were helping me with this issue.

However, I got confirmation that indeed they were working with me because I had an incredible angel reading with a young woman at the end of my seven days of working with the angels. At the end of the week, this young woman came for a private angel reading. I thought this was going to be my regular type of reading but, oh, no. The angels had a special thing in mind.

We started off talking about her angels in general, and I gave her their names. She came in with a list of items that she wanted to discuss, and the angels addressed each and every question. However, something special was about to happen. While I was telepathically receiving some information from her angels, they began to show me in my mind's eye an older man sitting on a huge granite rock. This had never happened before, but I trusted and went with the flow and allowed my angels to gently guide me.

This man seemed about 70 years old, was wearing a white shirt and green colored work pants with suspenders, and he had a black dog with him. I was getting the feeling and impression that he was her father. Not truly sure what was happening, I trusted and asked my client if her dad was deceased. She said, "Yes." I continued to explain to her what I was seeing, and she validated everything. I inquired about the black dog and she said that, yes, her dad had had a black Labrador Retriever. I made the statement that the dog was also deceased and she said, "Yes."

"Well," I said. "Your dad is here, just coming in to say hello and that he loves you very much and that the dog is with him keeping him company." This reading blew me away and permanently cured my fear of doing mediumship.

I slowly discovered just how powerful mediumship can be. Mediumship can help heal relationships or start someone or even a family on a healing path.

In 2002 when I was first starting out with readings and teaching, I remember one particular angel reading that I'd done at a center in upper New Hampshire. This far up in New Hampshire, it's difficult to find any metaphysical classes or shops.

There I was, trying out a new location for readings and possible classes. The community folks kept looking at me, trying to figure out what an angel reading was all about. I did have a few brave souls who took the plunge and scheduled a reading.

It was early afternoon when a young woman came in and began by telling me that she was a hairdresser and was just very curious about angels and especially about a reading. She explained that there was no one up in her area that did any of this. Once she finished, I started to talk to her about what an angel reading was and what she could possibly expect.

As I began to make my connection with her angels, I kept hearing inside of my head, "Wayne, Wayne, Wayne." This name did not feel like an angel or a spirit guide. It felt like a deceased loved one, but it did not feel like a family member. I was desperately trying to figure this one out, and then I finally gave up. This being was only giving me his name and that was it. So I trusted and moved ahead with the reading.

I told the young gal that I kept hearing the name "Wayne" inside my head and asked if this made any sense. She looked surprised. She said, "What? I can't believe that he showed up!" I said that this person's name is Wayne and that he is deceased. She said, "Yes, he is," and then explained that Wayne had been her sister's boyfriend. Sadly, he had killed her and then himself.

He was there to say that he was terribly sorry for all of the pain that he caused the family and that he was looking for forgiveness. More messages came in for the family. Wayne took the risk of coming in to assist this family on their healing journey and to help heal himself. To the spirit of Wayne, I say thank you for your messages of love, forgiveness and hope.

As you can see from this last reading, Wayne had a deep message to pass on with the intent of assisting the family in healing. In my work with angels, sometimes the spirit world needs to connect also to help.

This reminds me of another mediumship reading that I did a few years ago with a young man who came to me for a reading and some spiritual guidance. His name was Randy and he said that he was having a hard time with life. He had just moved back to the area to get his life together and wanted a reading. So we scheduled an appointment.

The moment I opened the door, I could clearly sense a huge cloud of darkness all around him. I quickly asked Archangel Michael to clear him so that we could begin. As he sat on the couch, he began to tell me that he was originally from the New England area, had moved to Texas and then to California, Colorado and back to Massachusetts. He was a chiropractor and a healer who was unemployed and looking for work.

As Randy spoke of his travels, his voice seemed so very far away. His angels already started to speak with me and told me to ask him about what had happened in Texas. His angels said that something had happened in Texas and that we needed to discuss this matter.

When he was finished, I said, "Randy, your angels tell me that something happened in Texas and they want you to tell me and that we need to talk about this. So what happened in Texas?" Randy looked stunned--like a deer caught in the headlights. You know this look.

He then said that he had been working in a health facility and they fired him. He ranted and raved about how they fired him. I heard and saw the anger in his voice and words, as he told me that he was in a lawsuit with this company. He was out for blood and wanted revenge. His angels came right in and told me to tell him to drop the legal suit because he was not going to win. Randy did not want to hear any of this. He said, "Those bastards are going to pay for what they did to me, and I am not dropping the lawsuit."

Just as he was fuming about all of this, his deceased father appeared. He stood just off to the left side of him and appeared to be upset with himself. His father told me that he was very sorry to see his son suffering this way, and that he, too, was here to apologize for all the wrongdoings in the family. He was sorry for causing his son grief. I could see Randy's deceased father crying. He was looking for understanding and forgiveness. He gave me the impression that he was spiritually stuck.

I asked Randy if his father was deceased and he said, "Yes." I told him that his father was here and wanted to say a few things. Randy did not want any part of this. He was a very angry young man and extremely angry with his father. Randy was gay and his father apparently did not understand or accept him.

I told Randy what his father was telling me. Randy's father's message was that he was sorry for treating him

84

that way. His father was truly sorry for the way in which he treated the whole family.

Randy chimed in, saying that his father had pitted everyone against everyone else in the family. There was no peace in the family. I could see Randy's father crying and saying that he was sorry. I shared this with Randy and he said, "My father is crying?" I concurred. "Good," Randy said with glee. "I am glad that he is unhappy and that he is upset. That bastard screwed up the whole family. He deserves what he gets and I really don't care about him." I could see and feel all the hate from an entire life spill from Randy's mouth and soul.

Not too much more was said, and Randy left the appointment an unchanged being. Bless his heart, and I hope he finds his way out of the anger and hate.

These are some examples of the power of mediumship and connecting with the spirit world. My fears around mediumship are now healed.

Chapter 15

BEING A DIVINE MESSENGER

I DEEPLY LOVE BEING A Divine messenger. I have learned that in being such a messenger, one may be required to give a heart-wrenching reading. My angel camp experience did not prepare me for the harshness of this reality.

While doing readings at a metaphysical shop in Massachusetts, I was approached by a young mother who desperately wanted an angel reading. She could not afford the fee, but my angels told me to help this person and to just gift her a reading.

She was 31 years old and very emotional. Her voice crackled when she spoke to me, and she appeared to be very nervous, even anxious. I asked her how I could help. "Oh, Elizabeth," she said, "I have a very sick little boy at home, and his name is Andrew." She continued to talk about Andrew and said that he was three years old and that he had been very sick since birth. As her eyes began to tear up a little, she continued to tell me that Andrew had had multiple surgeries since he was born. She said that she only had one important question to ask her angels and that question was, "Is Andrew going to be staying here with us?" My heart sank because the angels were already telling me, "No."

I knew this reading was going to be probably the most difficult reading I had ever given anybody. I asked for strong Divine assistance with this reading. Telepathically talking to my angels very quickly I told them that I did not have the heart to say "No" to a mother. It would break her heart. So I asked them to guide me to the deck of oracle cards that I had in front of me and help me choose the right cards that would tell the story.

I got clear guidance to use a certain fairy oracle card deck. I started to shuffle the cards (the angels work with me in a fascinating way with the cards), and as usual the cards just started sticking out of the deck. This is their way of telling me, "Here are the cards that you need." I was guided to three cards only from one deck, which I slowly laid down on the table. With a deep breath, I could see the whole story and how this was going to play out with her son.

Now it was my time to provide the complete message, and I asked the angels to lovingly guide me with the story and my words. Mary was looking very curious and anxious to hear what the angels had to say. I took another deep breath and I began the reading.

"Mary," I said, "the angels are telling me that you are going on a vacation fairly soon. Feels like the end of the month. They are giving me the feeling of an amusement park setting, and this trip is coming up fast." Mary acknowledged that they had a trip planned for Disney because Andrew so badly wanted to see Mickey Mouse. I said, "Good. Go, and I hope the whole family is going."

She said, "Yes, they are." It was going to be a whole-family event and fun for everyone, she continued. "Good," I said. "Just go and have a wonderful time and it's going to be a very important family affair."

I kept talking and telling Mary that the angels were explaining that very shortly after the vacation, Andrew was going to be given another opportunity to go home, if he chooses to. It felt like there was another medical appointment or possibly another surgery to be scheduled right after their trip. While looking at the last card, I continued to say that with the way Andrew was feeling right now, he was choosing to go back home. Tears streamed down Mary's face, and she reached into her handbag and pulled out a photo of Andrew. He was a sweet little boy with deep blue eyes and angel wings around him. Mary turned to me and said, "Elizabeth, you don't know Andrew, but he walks around home and pulls on me and says, "Mommy, it hurts too much to be here. I want to go home."

I started to tear up myself, and I thought, 'Here is a three-year-old who knows where home is. Isn't that interesting?' Then reality hit me. Not all readings were going to be light and easy. Some would be heart wrenching, yet all can provide opportunities to learn.

The reality is we are all here for just a short time, so let's enjoy life itself!

Chapter 16

ANGELS ON MY SHOULDERS

"**O**H, GOD, I'M GOING to be late. I have an angel party to do up in New Hampshire." Running around the house, I found everything that I needed and I was rushing off. I put my angels around my vehicle and me, and then I asked that they safely guide me on the road.

I love doing angel readings because, to me, it is a very sacred and special experience. For a short time, I get to see someone's soul journey and their challenges and life lessons.

Yet, while driving, I was feeling some heaviness inside of me, and this told me that the evening would be a rough one. Probably some intense angel readings would be required tonight.

In staying positive, I listened to soft new age music in the car and just told the angels to get me there on time. I arrived at the house party on time, with a few extra minutes to spare. There were two other readers and myself, and the people had already started coming in.

After I created sacred space in the room where I was

going to do my readings, I prepared myself with prayer and meditation and I began the readings. My intuition was right and that indeed there would be some intense emotional readings that night.

One woman (I'll call her Sally) came to me with a big smile on her face. She was so excited about connecting with her angels and could hardly keep still.

I started to talk with her about angels in general, explaining what they were. Then I described who was around her and gave her the angels' names. She was thrilled to know that she had two large angels. As I spoke softly to her about her angels, the angels began nudging me to ask her questions about her children.

So I told her that her angels wanted to talk about her children and I said that they were showing me the number two, meaning two children. "Yes," she said excitedly. "Yes, I have two children." She was so excited that she offered to show me their pictures. Sally grabbed her handbag and pulled out one picture of her children. Both were in the picture together. One was around 8 or 9 years old, and the other was around 6 or 7 years old.

As I looked at the picture, the angels brought my attention to the older one, who I will call Cameron. I explained to Sally that the angels wanted to talk about the older of the two little boys. She was surprised in one way, but not in another. Cameron had been diagnosed with leukemia and was receiving chemotherapy. He was having a hard time with the treatments. Then the angels gently told me that he was here for only a short time. I asked if I needed to share that information with the mother and they said, "Yes."

I was not sure how to approach this matter so I quickly asked Archangel Michael for courage and guidance, and then I asked Archangel Gabriel to help open my throat chakra so that I may speak from a place of love and compassion. I knew that they would assist me in delivering this heart-breaking message of love.

Sally had become very settled and serious. Her smile was gone, and she desperately wanted to know what the angels had to say about her son Cameron. At this point, I would have liked to have passed up this type of reading or just run the other way. But I knew I had a job to do, and I felt reassured that my angelic team would divinely guide me through it.

I inquired about Cameron's progress, and she said in a very low and soft voice that he was struggling. He was having a hard time with the chemotherapy and that all of her time was being spent at the hospital. At this point the angels chimed in and told me that she was not living, and with all of the extra care and time she had been giving Cameron, her youngest son was being neglected (not physically, but emotionally). This family wasn't living life but was just going through the motions of life itself.

I gently explained that the angels had said Cameron was only going to be here for a short time. Sally started getting very upset and was getting angry with God. "How could God do this to my son? Elizabeth, why would God put a little child through all this pain and suffering, and now you're telling me that Cameron is going to die regardless of all the prayers that I have been saying?" Sally's tears were streaming down her face, and my own heart was sinking along with hers.

I kept centered and focused and asked the angels to help me even more. They began to explain to me that sometimes a soul comes in for a short time to have a more intense effect on people. For this family, Cameron was the brave little soul who decided to come in for a short time to help bring a separated family back together again. Once news had gotten out about Cameron, the whole family had rallied together.

Cameron made a soul decision and contract long before, to assist these other souls in this family, just as we are all here to assist each other on our own sacred journey.

I attempted to explain what the angels were saying, but she could not hear me. I tried to tell her that our timeline for events is different from that of the angels. In truth, Cameron is a little boy in physical appearance only. But spiritually, he is a very wise, old and brave soul who made a commitment to help his family move through old unforgiveness and anger.

During the reading, even though my heart was pounding and feeling very nervous, I could sense the angels all around. It felt like they were sitting on my shoulder whispering to me all the right words and guidance that I needed to give.

After the reading, I thanked my angelic team for their assistance and, last I knew, Cameron is alive and still fighting his leukemia.

Chapter 17

MY ENCOUNTER WITH THE NATURE ANGELS

DO YOU BELIEVE IN nature angels or, I should say, fairies? I know that the subject of fairies may seem very "far out there" and maybe it is, but I have had some personal encounters with fairies. Fairies are also called devas and the nature angels. They are usually small--about one inch tall--but I have also seen a fairy as large as six feet tall. Yes, six feet tall and I saw it up in the mountains of New Hampshire.

When I attended angel camp, the teacher spoke to us about the nature angels. I said to myself, "Hmmm . . . fairies." I was not really sure if they truly exist, but I listened very carefully to what was being said in class.

Shortly after I returned home from the training, I was guided to spend some time in nature. I love nature and plants and especially animals, who at times seem to me more nurturing than people.

As I walked along my favorite nature path just enjoying the scenery, and taking it all in, my thoughts drifted to the question of fairies and whether they really exist.

While walking, I decided I wanted some company, so I called in my angels and Christ to walk with me, asking at the same time that if the fairies were real to give me a clear, concrete sign that day. I stopped and looked all around, expecting to get a sign right away, but none was forthcoming. I waited a couple of minutes and then continued on the nature path. I did not know what to expect but just kept looking.

About three-quarters of the way down the path, I was unexpectedly guided to take a different path. This one was off the beaten trail and more secluded. I began to feel very sad because most of the trees and forest in this area were badly burned by fire. I was not sure what actually happened, but I looked all around and could only see black. Just about everything was severely burned and charcoal black.

Continuing on this new path, I came to an open field, and the fire had affected that area, as well. The sun was now on my back and the sky was a beautiful blue above me. When I looked up I noticed a butterfly coming my way and squinted to see what kind of butterfly it was but could not identify it. It was too high up for me to see but came closer and closer then circled right above my head and started flying in the other direction.

I turned to watch it leave, mentally calling out to it, asking the butterfly to come back so I could see its wings. But it kept flying away from me and I gave up and turned to face the trail again. Then, quite suddenly, a butterfly landed on my right shoulder. I could see its shape and wings in my shadow, but every time I tried to look at it, the butterfly moved slightly down my shoulder, away from my central focus of vision.

So I allowed the butterfly to just rest on my shoulder, still able to see in silhouette that it was sunning its wings, soaking up all the good sunshine rays. Finally, my curiosity got the best of me. I quickly turned to look and heard it fly away but never saw it leave. The butterfly just seemed to vanish without a trace. Everything around me was burnt, so it was not hard to miss a beautiful butterfly, and though I kept looking, I never saw it again. I was totally baffled by the whole experience, but didn't realize that this had been my sign until much later that evening.

While taking a shower I remembered that the butterfly was symbolic of the fairy realm! One of the fairy oracle card decks I have even has a butterfly on the cover of each of the cards. 'Oh my God,' I thought. I was screaming in my head that I *did* get a sign and I needed to share this with someone.

Quickly I jumped out of the shower and called my brother Rick in California and told him my fairy story and explained that I had been looking for some validation.

"Well, sis" he said, "I have even a better story to tell you and even more validation." Something strange had happened that same day for him.

My brother plays the organ and sings at a local church in California. He proceeded to tell me that the priest of the parish handed him an envelope that same day and said that this was his belated Easter bonus for playing at the church. Rick said that this envelope that the priest gave him was unusual. The envelope had a picture of a butterfly on the outside. Once he opened the envelope, he found that his bonus money was wrapped up in stationery. It was stationery that was all covered with butterflies. 'How weird,' my brother thought. He had been playing for the church for quite some time now, and he had received bonuses before--but never in a fancy envelope and never wrapped in stationery.

We both got validation that same day.

As time went on, I began to feel fairies around me. Several months later, I took my camera and ventured to ask the fairies to please show themselves to me, and one did. His name is "Willow".

Another very unique fairy experience occurred in 2003. It happened all so innocently. I was in Goshen, New Hampshire at a place called "On Top of the Mountain," teaching a class on creating prosperity with the angels. While the students were completing a money exercise, I was looking around at the class just to see where everyone was in terms of finishing the exercise. While looking to my right to check on the students on that side of the room, quite suddenly, I saw standing behind one of the students, a six-foot pink fairy. Yes, a six-foot pink fairy! She was simply gorgeous all pink, covered in glitter and light, with beautiful long arms and legs, a cameo face and huge butterfly wings that sparkled.

Pardon my French, but I said to myself, "Holy shit." In fact, I said it twice because I could not believe what I was seeing. I had never heard of fairies being that big. I had always imagined that they were small . . . boy, was I wrong, I thought, wishing I had my camera.

I asked her who she was, and all she would tell me was that she was the fairy of the forest, not giving me her name. But seeing her this big, all I could think was that she held some very important role among the fairies and elemental world.

Then she telepathically spoke to me.

98

I quickly grabbed some paper and started to write. This pink fairy said, "Humans have a hard time manifesting wealth and abundance because of their beliefs and feelings around prosperity and abundance." She then walked through the class and walked right out of the building. What wonderful validation this was for me, because this is what I was teaching in this money class.

Seeing a six-foot pink fairy seemed pretty "out there," and I wanted some validation myself. I wasn't yet willing to just blurt out to the whole class about the pink fairy or what she had told me and quietly asked Linda, the owner of the place, if she had a pink fairy that comes to visit now and then. Linda replied, "Oh yes, she visits from time to time." I thought, Okay. I am going to ask now about how big this fairy is. "Linda," I said, "is this pink fairy big by any chance?" "Oh my God, yes, Elizabeth--about six feet tall," Linda exclaimed.

"Linda, I saw her and she came into the class and gave us a message about prosperity" I blurted out. Everyone's eyes lit up, and they all had this look of amazement on their face. Linda was gleeful and grateful that someone else had seen the pink fairy. Then Linda asked, "Elizabeth did you see her broken wing?" I thought about her question then replied "Sorry, but no I did not. I was so caught up in the color, sparkles and beauty that I did not notice anything broken." I shared the fairy's message with the class, and the class ended on a wonderful note.

A few weeks after the prosperity class, I received an email from Linda. She wrote in her email that she had been teaching an energy class, when one of the students was strongly guided to write a message down for Linda. The message did not make any sense to the student, but Linda almost fell off her chair.

This student knew nothing about the pink fairy, nor was she even a part of the prosperity class that I taught. But the message went like this: "In the times of King Arthur, fairies and elves were as large as humans, and the broken wing was caused by a fight with a dragon."

After reading this message, I almost fell off my chair, too. What marvelous validation this was for both Linda and me!

I saw the pink fairy again up there during another class, and was getting used to seeing her there. Then several months later she appeared in my mind's eye late one night while I was at home, responding to emails. This totally surprised me.

The fairy of the forest just appeared and told me that she could not stay too much longer and that she would be leaving. When I asked why, she showed me the land (what land I do not know), and I saw what looked like gray and black smoke slithering across it. I think that this smoke represented old emotional toxins and fear from people. The energy of the land was shifting. I have never seen her again after this last message. I am hoping she is in good hands.

May God bless the nature angels!

Chapter 18

MY RELATIONSHIP WITH THE DIVINE MOTHER

WHEN I WAS IN my teens and continuing into my early twenties, I used to talk with Jesus and the Blessed Mother or Mother Mary. My favorite time and place to pray and talk to them was while I was taking a bath. It was my time, and I could very easily quiet my mind and focus with intention on what I wanted to talk to them about.

I talked to them about everything, and then one day when I was around my early- to mid- twenties, I told them that I did not need them any more. I felt that there were other people who needed their help more than I did. I told them that there were families who were living out on the streets, kids and elderly dying in hospitals. They needed their help more than I did.

At the time, I did not realize that the angels, and especially the Masters like Christ and Mother Mary, could be with everyone all at the same time. What did I know at the age of 20? Apparently, I was very naïve, and when I said that I did not need their help any more, it was at that point that I severed my connection with the Divine.

I did not realize how much my life was going to spiral down, and when it did, I feverishly started to pray again. I wanted my connection back, and it happened very slowly. God's connection to us is always present and perfect. However, it is our connection back to God that needs work and strengthening. My full connection did not happen until I was around 43 years old. It is amazing to me that it took over twenty years for me to find my way back.

I always felt close to the Divine Mother, and she has always been very special to me. Many times when I need some extra tender loving care (TLC) and support, she is always right there by my side. She is the Ascended Master who represents Divine Compassion.

One day in the summer of 2004, I was working at home and the phone was ringing off the hook. People needed appointments, information on classes, and more. I was on the phone literally from 1-4 pm, with no pause. I began to panic because I was offering a new class on angels and ascended masters that was going to be starting in three weeks, and I had nothing prepared. I did not even know how I was going to present the information or what masters wanted to be a part of this class.

"Okay," I said to myself. "Enough is enough. I need some time out." I decided right then and there that I was going to run away from home and the office for a little while. I packed up some angel books, pen, pad of paper and my beach blanket and then headed out to the ocean.

I arrived late in the afternoon, but I didn't care. I walked all the way down towards the end of the beach where it was less populated, laid my blanket out and just relaxed for a bit.

Then I grabbed one of my angel books and began to read. I was hoping to start getting ideas about this new class. While reading and jotting down some notes, the face of the Blessed Mother appeared very clearly in my mind's eye. She did not say anything, but I asked if she wanted to be a part of the angel and ascended master study group. She was not saying anything, so I asked if it was important for people to begin to know her more and work with her. Again, she did not say anything, or at least I did not hear anything. When this happens, I bring out my secret weapon for getting validation.

I told the Blessed Mother that if she wanted to be a part of this study group and if it was important for people to know her better and to work with her, then I needed a direct sign from her. I told her that I wanted a heart-shaped stone today, which would be a concrete sign from her validating that she indeed was supposed to be a part of the study group. I don't usually ask for a specific sign, but this was something that I truly wanted.

I set my intention and then let go of it. Her face disappeared, and I went back to my book and note-taking.

After about a half-hour of reading, I decided to stretch my legs and walk down towards the water. I thought I would also do some exploring, which is one of my favorite things to do.

As I started to make my way down to the water, about fourteen feet from my blanket, I came across a pile of stones. I decided to go and check this out. It seemed that someone was trying to build a stone castle. Nice job, but they had not completed it.

A few feet from this stone castle, my eye caught sight of

a stone, which was half buried in the sand. There was nothing unusual about this stone, but I was guided over to it. I dug around it and pulled it out of the sand. As I brushed off the excess dirt and sand, I turned it over and saw that the stone was a perfect heart-shaped stone with a cross in the middle.

I didn't have the words back then, and still don't have the right words today. But my heart filled with joy and bliss at the same time, and I told the Blessed Mother, "Thank you for this wonderful gift."

In many ways, this was the best gift ever, and I still have this heart-shaped stone sitting right near my bed today. It is a gentle yet powerful reminder of the Blessed Mother's love for me and for all.

Deeply touched by this special gift of love, this whole experience moved me into a much deeper connection with the Divine and into a deeper understanding of my own spirituality.

While getting ready to leave the beach, I was thinking to myself about how I was doing spiritually when something magical happened. Another sign was given to me on my way back to the car. I came upon a sandcastle that was three-quarters completed. This sign was a powerful visual validation of my spiritual growth and progress and the direction in which I was going.

For the rest of the day, I was in a state of bliss and gratitude, and I knew that the Divine Mother was dwelling in my heart and soul and was also walking with me on my path.

Chapter 19

ANGELS IN ALASKA

I NEVER KNOW IN ADVANCE how I will be used in Divine service, but looking back I can see that God and angels had plans for me to serve and as always, to learn in Alaska.

In the fall of 2004, I sponsored Lee Carroll who channels an inter-dimensional being named "Kryon." I was taking care of all the workshop registration when someone from Anchorage, Alaska emailed me about attending the workshop. "Wow!" I thought, "Alaska! Now that would be a nice place to visit and to the see the aurora borealis."

So I took the liberty of also inquiring about doing some angel workshops in Anchorage. This woman thought that it might be a possibility and that we could talk when she came up for the event.

On the day of the Kryon event, I met up with this young woman from Alaska though we only had time to speak briefly. However, we connected about a month later and she put me in touch with some other people in Anchorage who run a wellness magazine and holistic festival.

After writing an angel article for their new age magazine and registering for the festival, I began to make my travel plans to Anchorage. I must honestly admit, I was nervous. Not knowing anyone over there, I had to trust my Divine guidance for I knew that I needed to make this trip. I had several talks with my good friend Allison - she was great at calming me down and helping me to refocus. I am deeply indebted to her wise and loving advice and Divine guidance.

My travel plans were completed in February 2005, and everything was coming together nicely. However, people in Alaska were not yet signing up for any of my classes. So I was getting nervous but kept hearing relax and that everything would be just fine. I was getting worried about the money because this was going to be an expensive trip. Again, my good friend and spiritual mentor Allison came to the rescue and was able to calm me down and remind me that I was doing God's work and failure was not an option in God's world.

It was about the beginning of March 2005 when I received a beautiful email from Allison. She eagerly wrote in her email to me that she found a channeling message on the Internet, done by one of the Aleut Elders in Alaska. Allison said that she found it to be interesting because in certain sections, this elder talks about angels. In fact, the channeled message said, "a host of angels is coming through Alaska to help anchor in the Divine Feminine Energy...." (to view full article go to www.goodworksonearth.org/larry-merculieff-let-goodness-take-its-place.html).

This was truly a beautiful message in the Aleut language to the natives and people of Alaska. The channeled message said, "the center of the top of the energy entrance to the Earth Mother is here through Alaska. The spiritual leaders say that a host of angels is coming through Alaska-- spreading out throughout the world for this healing to take place."

While reading this message, I got goose bumps all over; I knew that something was going to take place while I was in Alaska. I was beginning to sense that my trip would serve a larger purpose. Still uncertain about just what that would be, and despite having stray moments of anxiety, my trust in my inner guidance about Alaska grew.

The mountains in Alaska are glorious and were definitely worth my long trip. I almost felt like I was in heaven looking at these mighty powerful and majestic mountains that surround all of Anchorage.

The people of Alaska are quite interesting. All too soon I discovered that many I met seemed to have come to Alaska to somehow escape life. The energy of Alaska felt dense and heavy and I knew that there was a lot of work to be done while I was there.

My schedule included offering angel readings, a few mini angel classes and later the Angel Reader certification program. I was there for two weeks and by the start of the second week, I could feel my own energy dropping and getting heavier.

Before I started with readings at a whole health festival, I took a walk outside the hotel where I was staying and where the festival was taking place. I wanted some time just for me, to reinforce my own connection to the Divine. While walking around Hood Lake, I was suddenly guided to walk over to a small green shack-like building and I discovered it was a water protection shed near the lake.

So crossing the street I walked around to the right side and towards the front of the shed. I am very curious about everything and I just wanted to check this building out.

While walking towards the front of the shed, I happened to look down and saw, mixed in with all the dead grass and old fall leaves, a stone mostly buried under all the grass and sticks and leaves, but I could make out a small hand carved in the stone.

I cleared away the entire area and cleaned all the dirt and debris from the stone. Then I saw it fully. A beautiful hand-crafted stone with two hands in prayer mode. The message went like this: "Until We Meet Again Find Peace in Heavens Hands." This was a goose bumps moment!

What a beautiful message and what a strange place to find this stone plaque I thought. It reminded me of a flat tomb stone. Perhaps an animal was buried there, but I loved the message, and my spirits lifted and I returned to the hotel.

During the readings, I began to see a bigger picture of the challenges of the Alaskan people. Many are still functioning from their root and sacral chakra energy meaning that they were living more in survival mode and interested in their physical challenges. However, others were trying to spiritually ignite their soul.

The angel readings were quite varied, and compassionately addressed each person's needs. One client in particular told me that, "The reading was all so nice and it was great to hear what the angels had to say, but, Elizabeth, when am I going to have sex again with my true soulmate?" You might think that this question would have shocked me, but in truth I think I have heard it all. The angels are never shocked by our words and they always reply in a graceful manner.

I explained to this client who is looking for her soulmate that, according to the angels, she had some work to do first and that there was someone out there for her, but it would be another year and a half before her soulmate would present himself. She was not happy with this and became very frustrated. We ended the session shortly after this message both aware that if she was up to the challenge this could bring more positive changes to her life.

For many that came for a reading, their love life was the main theme. Very few inquired about their spiritual path or wanted to know how to communicate more with their own angels.

However, there were some very powerful souls who just needed a jump-start. I kept getting some messages that there were just going to be a small hand-full at first doing this work, and that they need some self-confidence to get them moving.

One young man I remember clearly approached me for a reading at the health festival. During his reading, his angels told me that he was tired of being here, that this human life was very hard for him, and that he was wishing he could just go home.

I gently imparted to him this information from his angels and he looked completely shocked because his angels were right on the money with their message. He honestly admitted that he fantasized about moving on and out...checking out that is. He was divorced and struggling to find a soulmate and to be at peace. He said that he has never experienced peace and love in his life.

His angels spoke more and wanted to let him know about his energy and how his thoughts create his reality. I tried to explain this in a way that made some sense to him, as this was a new revelation.

The angels came in very strong and loud and said that if he did not make some necessary changes in his life, he would get his wish very shortly. In my spiritual work I find that when the angels come in with a message that is very abrupt, it usually means that this person needs to take action right away.

This was very true in his case. When I returned home, there was a message already waiting for me from a gal who helped me with my classes. She left me a message saying that he had been trying to reach me, that he had been rushed to the hospital the very day that I left Alaska.

He was bleeding internally and lost three quarters of his total volume blood in his body. The doctors had to quickly infuse him and were amazed that he was even alive after losing most of his blood.

I sent him angels and healing energy. He is fine today and hopefully working towards finding peace within himself.

God and angels knew I had my work cut out for me so they gifted me with a very special and unique present just before I left.

During the Angel Healing Practitioner Program, a student name Mari approached me and said that she was going to be doing a channeling session later that evening and invited me to come. I was delighted and then asked whom was she going to be channeling? She said that she channels various masters including Mother Mary but she said tonight is a message from the star people, more specifically, the Pleiadians (these are the star people who are very powerful healers and peacemakers and their home is Pleiades, which is in our solar system).

At first I thought, "Rats! I came all the way to Alaska to hear the Pleiadians!? Well okay..."

However, the angels had a surprise waiting for me during the channeling, one that I will never forget.

When everyone had finished the first day of the angel program, I headed off to dinner. I kept thinking about the channeling session that I would be attending shortly, and thought, "Hey what the heck. I usually don't sit in on channeling sessions and it certainly beats just sitting in my hotel room."

I returned with a positive attitude, found the best seat in the house, and was open to the experience of the Pleiadians. I personally or even professionally didn't know of anyone who channels the Pleiadians so this would at least be interesting

It was a small gathering of people, but I thought that it was perfect. My gift of clairvoyance had become much stronger over time and I had developed the ability to see auras and energy around a person. Mari's aura was beautiful but when the channeling began, her whole energy field shifted dramatically. The Pleiadians also put on one heck of a light show and they even mentioned that during the channeling.

Different colors of energy and even shooting stars were visible to my naked eye. The Pleiadians were very playful and even charming.

But then suddenly, the Pleiadians said that there was someone else who wanted to come in. Once again I was intrigued to see Mari's aura shift and change though I didn't understand what it all meant.

Mari's aura changed to a complete pink bubble that surrounded her whole body. This pink energy then stretched over and formed another pink bubble of light right across from Mari and, you guessed it. This new energy was Mother Mary also known as Miriam who was Jesus' mother. I had never seen this before. It looked like there were two beings. One was Mari and the other someone else.

The messages from Mary were a wonderfully beautiful

surprise for me. I felt truly blessed by this whole experience and what a lovely way to end my trip here in Alaska!

Yes, there are angels in Alaska and my big lesson here was to trust my Divine guidance and to hold compassion for all.

Chapter 20

FACING MY FEARS

MUCH OF MY LIFE I never felt like I fitted in or even belonged anywhere, and there are moments even now when I still feel this way. Many of my students say "Elizabeth, you are a great teacher and you teach with such ease, grace and confidence," unaware of the personal struggle and metamorphosis that I had to go through in order to follow my calling.

Until now, few have known about my fears, anxieties, doubts and lack of confidence that kept me a prisoner most of my life.

Being a Lightworker, a spiritual teacher, healer and mentor requires much change not only for me but also for anyone who is called to serve.

Many times I even questioned my own ability to grasp spiritual concepts, be open to my intuition, trust and teach others. I had no idea of my spiritual path or what was going to happen. There were fears of speaking in public. Having had several severe anxiety attacks in school, I shied away from the spot light and public speaking.

I vividly remember in graduate school, I was studying epidemiology and we had to work in groups of five people. The assignment was to design a clinical trial and present the study to the whole class of about 40 people. My group designed a caffeine study and I diligently researched the topic and worked on my piece of the project. I wrote out my whole talk, which was about three minutes, on index cards. I thought I would be all right if I read my part of the presentation from the cards. On the day of our group presentation, I was nervous (I did not know about the angels back then) and full of fear. I was fearful of what others would think and of being judged. I so badly wanted to do a good job because most of our grade was resting on the presentation and now I was worried about letting my whole group down.

Well, when it was finally my turn, I started out reading the first sentence from my index cards.

At the half-way point of the second sentence, my anxiety level sky rocketed to the point that I could not speak anymore or even breathe. Everyone was looking at me, and I felt so dumb and stupid that I could not even bear to look at anyone. I gave one of my team members my index card with all the information on it and they had to read it for me. I could feel my heart pounding and felt totally ashamed and embarrassed.

The two professors who were co-teaching the class did not know how to respond. It was a very awkward moment for everyone, including me. Both professors came over to me afterward and said "nice job" in a very loving way. I thought to myself, "You have got to be kidding me. Nice job my foot."

My performance was lousy and I felt like a total failure. That same day I made a vow to never do another public presentation again. Public speaking was too humiliating to me and I never wanted to put myself in that position again.

After being angelically pushed into teaching and holding workshops, I had to rise above my fear of speaking in public. I tried deep breathing and anti-anxiety medications like Xanax, and Valium. Nothing worked. I could still physically and emotionally experience the torment that my anxiety brought me.

After consulting my physician, he prescribed a beta-blocker, which is normally given for hypertension, but it does inhibit the physical symptoms of anxiety like the pounding heart and butterflies in the stomach. This worked perfectly! Finally some relief! What a wonderful feeling, I could now lecture without any worries! Just being able to focus on doing my work without feeling anxious was a blessing.

One day I decided to have a heart to heart conversation with Archangel Michael. I shared with Michael the love and passion I felt about teaching and my concerns about being dependent on a medication. Totally beside myself and feeling like being stuck between a rock and a hard place, Michael gave me an idea that could help me with my public speaking anxiety and remove the emotional dependency on a medication.

Michael instructed me to use him as my anti-anxiety medication. So when I start feeling anxious and worried about what people will think, I invoke Archangel Michael and tell him just how I am feeling. Then I give him permission to enter my body, calm it down and restore peace of mind and harmony. Within seconds it is done! Gentle energy flows over me like a waterfall and I can feel all the anxiety leaving my body and my mind becoming very calm and focused. My secret anti-anxiety weapon is Archangel Michael! He is a wonderful tranquilizer! He gives confidence and peace where there is doubt and anxiety.

That was more than five years ago and look at me now. I am speaking to many different kinds of groups, teaching throughout the United States and feeling more confident than ever. Working with Archangel Michael and my spiritual team has helped me to face my fears, and I am forever grateful!

Chapter 21

DARK NIGHT OF THE SOUL

I ALWAYS THOUGHT THAT SOMEONE could only experience one dark night of the soul, and as time went on, I discovered I was very wrong.

All the assorted jobs in my life provided me with wonderful opportunities for self-reflection and growth. Many times I had jobs whereby I was forced to work with very negative, self-centered and egotistical people. Some had egos the size of the universe and their words were as sharp as a razor's edge.

Several times I have questioned my own ability as a spiritual teacher. Of course, I thought, "Who am I to teach others about angels or about their spirituality? I do not have a Ph.D. I am not a published author!" What credentials did I have that would demonstrate a level of knowledge or an area of expertise that I believed I needed to show the world that I was worthy of teaching about angels and other spiritual topics?

Many struggles with self-esteem and self-worth were right in my face. I saw everyone else as being smarter, more creative and intuitive and gifted. Several times, I would wonder, what could I possibly offer anyone? My life here is not that important and I am not that unique.

Because my self-esteem had been so badly injured in growing up, I have a tendency toward a "take a look at what I have done" attitude. My spiritual maturity is now asking me to practice random and silent acts of kindness. In the past I did not like taking responsibility for my actions and just blamed others and when in victim mode, blame and whine. Now it is imperative for me to be responsible for everything (actions, feelings, intentions and outcomes) and to move away from the "Hey, take a look at me" mentality.

As I started growing my spiritual business, I had such doubts and lack of confidence I did not know what to do at times. Numerous times I wanted to throw in the towel and just say forget about the angels and my path. The challenges were too hard and I did not have the faith in myself.

While teaching an angel class at a small metaphysical center in Massachusetts, many of the participants thanked me after the class. They said, 'Elizabeth this was wonderful. You're so gifted and you made learning fun. You brought the concepts of angels down to Earth, and thank you!"

Everyone felt touched by their angels, truly feeling elated that they made a contact with their guardian angels.

After giving hugs and saying good-bye to all, I slowly began to gather my things and shut off the lights in the room. I was the last person to leave the building and had the responsibility of locking up the center.

As I shut off the light in the workshop room, I finished gathering my belongings and began to silently cry to myself. I was feeling like a total fake and phony. I could hear myself saying, "Who do you think you are to teach people about angels? You tell people that they can see them but you're not even sure you can see them. You're not that enlightened, super psychic and you were not born into a metaphysical family. You tell people about their angels and teach them how to make their connection when in fact you're not even sure of your own connection."

As I sat quietly on the floor, I was heavily sobbing and feeling so sorry for myself. I was contemplating the idea of giving up teaching all together when I could feel a large presence behind me. I was feeling too beside myself to even care if this presence was a good energy or not. I just didn't care anymore. My ego was having a field day with me.

Still crying, I could hear inside of my head, "Pick yourself up, brush yourself off for tomorrow is a better day." My tears were so strong that I didn't care what was being said. I even began to argue with this being saying, "You don't understand! I am a fake and a phony, and I am not sure of anything."

The voice spoke again only now louder and in a very firm tone. "Pick yourself up, brush yourself off for tomorrow is a better day."

So I picked myself up and dusted myself off. While driving home and still crying, I began questioning my own path and what direction I was headed in. Mentally exhausted, I opted to just sleep on it for the night and, just maybe the next day really would be better.

I asked the angels and Archangel Michael to help me to lift my spirits and, upon awakening the next morning, I did indeed feel better and now ready to teach another class. I never doubted my teaching path again!

I am very disciplined and am determined to assist those who choose to discover their own Divinity, inner truth and can bring out the very best in others and empower them.

While walking this spiritual path, I must be constantly

aware of my dependency of looking outside of myself for validation of self-worth, success and love. I had to learn to face my fear and even partnership with my fear to turn fears into a creative force that can be used positively.

Stubbornness is another challenge for me. As I strive to be more flexible and open to change, I free myself. The stubbornness must be the Taurus in me.

I am not PERFECT! But my deep spiritual awakening has led me to be aware of my challenges or traps. I must listen when God speaks and know the great love and power that I am.

Do I still have some dark night of the soul experiences? You bet, from time to time. I am now able to move through these periods with more ease and grace. These moments are just moments now they do not paralyze me anymore.

The bringing together of the sum of my human/spiritual existence was necessary for me to stay focused on my path and continue the spiritual work that I had embarked on. From all the negative overlays, I felt that my Higher Self or God-Self was totally separate. I knew I had to bring them back together in more unison if I was going to be supported on this new path-the infusion of my Higher Self or God-Self.

As Christine Page, MD author of Spiritual Alchemy said, "only when we surrender false identities and cease power games can we reach inside and love, accept and integrate those parts of ourselves which are held separated by fear. As we accept ourselves we allow others to be exactly who they are."

If you stay in fear mode and are not open to change, this can lead to stagnation of the soul. People mirror back to us our strengths as well as our weaknesses. The mirror allows one to catch glimpses of who they truly are.

From time to time we have moments of truth and dark nights of the soul. And this is when we need to gently listen to the voice of our soul, for the soul knows only Love is real!

Chapter 22

MERGING WITH MY HIGHER SELF

E ARLY IN 2002, IN my unending quest for learning, I traveled to Texas to attend a special gathering. For me it was a wonderful blessing to have this opportunity and I firmly set my intent for deep spiritual growth.

Though the workshop itself proved interesting and it was truly beautiful to witness spiritual change in others, the profound experiences they had, and which I had hoped and prepared for, somehow seemed to escape me.

At the end of it all, my only deep personal experience was bone deep exhaustion and, I reluctantly admitted to myself, disappointment.

Deciding I was too worn out to even try to focus on these feelings until I was rested, I couldn't wait to get home again.

While sitting at the airport to return home, I was so tired that I pulled up my large suitcase and started to rest my head on it. Strangely, I could see out of the corner of my eye a streaking ball of white energy heading right towards me. This ball of energy came from the sky and moved very quickly through the air, passed right though the huge airport window, streaked passed everyone and, as I watched, this ball of pure white light came closer and closer, then hit my body. My physical body jerked and I fell fast asleep.

Too exhausted to even question or care about what just happened, little did I realize that this was but the beginning of the deep experience I so desired!

A couple months later, I had one of those funny dreams. You know the one where you think you're asleep but you feel that you're actually awake.

During this dream, I found myself in a very large brick building with windows. The kind of building that reminds you of an old factory building. This was my place of work and my two bosses, who I was working for in reality, were also in my dream. They came in to talk to me about a research project that I was working on.

I told them that I had a picture of an angel. Both were interested in seeing it. As I pulled out this picture I tried to focus on the photo but had a difficult time. So I took the picture to one of the windows in my office and had some light shine on it hoping that I could see the picture more clearly.

While looking at it, the photo changed right before my eyes. It was no longer a picture of an angel, but the photo had transformed into a huge white cloud with beautiful loving eyes in the middle just looking right at me. I screamed out loud "My God, this is God in the picture."

As quickly as my words flowed out of my mouth, I was transported back home, standing at the door entrance of my bedroom. My room looked exactly like it does in real life. While standing at the doorway, I saw myself lying in bed. Still observing from the doorway, within seconds of seeing myself in bed, I saw a huge, strong, solid beam of white light blazing down and penetrating my physical body. My whole body quickened and shook with energy and my arms started to rise up like I was reaching for something or someone. I could see that my physical body was being infused with more light and knew that a higher spiritual consciousness was being delivered. My Higher Self was becoming more integrated with the human angel that I was becoming.

The energy was so intense, that it woke me from my sleep. When I fully woke up, my whole body was shaking. This experience took me by surprise, yet at the time I still did not fully understand its meaning. Only later did I develop a deeper appreciation as I felt more and more my own Higher Self was making its presence known as the months passed. Welcoming that connection and integration, I have come to greatly value my Higher Self and the wisdom that it holds for me.

So! What is *really* meant by the words "Higher Self"?

Higher Self is that part of us that resides in the higher levels of one's experience. It is one's true awareness and God connection. There can be many layers of the Higher Self (soul, Oversoul or Higher Self) which represents different aspects of spiritual consciousness. It is the animating force within each of us that guides and directs our lower selves to search for higher understanding, meaning and expression, and to ultimately reach the state of transformation of becoming a fully integrated multi-dimensional being of light.

In simple terms, the Higher Self is the Christ Self, the I

AM presence and the exalted form of selfhood that contains all the light, wisdom and love of the God force.

I once believed that everyone was born with their full spiritual consciousness. However, over time I have come to believe and see that there is a delivery of spiritual energy to human beings which depends on the level of spiritual awakening, awareness and knowledge that each person attains in a given life-time.

As we attain mastery over our mental and emotional bodies and learn to temper these bodies with Divine Love, a stronger delivery of spiritual consciousness occurs.

Several years have passed since this experience and I am feeling stronger and see in my mind's eye light emanating from my physical body. From aura photos taken most recently, my aura has more white light woven through. White light in the aura represents a being that is transcending the physical and working with energies from a higher dimension and is on a deep spiritual path.

I am also sensing a pulling back or a stepping back of my spiritual team. I have been told by spirit, that the time has come for many to hold their own power and to know their own power. The torch of light is being handed to humans now. As placeholders of the light, as a strong group of souls, we are being asked to step into our own power and light and hold the sacred energies of the land and burn our light brightly.

We are all becoming human angels and awakening to our own divinity.

Chapter 23

PERSONAL
METAMORPHOSIS

MY DEAR BELOVED FRIEND and spiritual colleague Allison, whom I'd met at Angel Camp, can give some amazing readings and is probably the only person who can give me a reading with profound messages. From time to time, I call Allison and ask her to do a mini reading for me, especially when I have much going on and have trouble focusing.

I would like to share with you a reading that she did for me earlier in 2005. First I thought I would get a lecture about taking better care of myself and taking time for myself. However, the Masters and Angels had another entirely different message for me. It was one that I needed to read over and over, just to make sure that I got it all. So here is the message I received from heaven . . .

"Dear Elizabeth, you have great leadership ability and are practical, and these abilities must be developed to their fullest. You will need your strong constitution to get the clear message to your unwilling hearer.

You were chosen early, and learned to rely on the Divine Mother then--as you must now. Her appearance in your life and presence for these past months has been to strengthen you, and your closeness with her is your true motherly support--precisely for challenges to come in various ways, as well as particularly with your earthly mother.

Here is the moment of and opportunity for change for the better in your mental and emotional life! Reach out to those who care for you for support. Use your ability for fairness for your personal healing--that is, be fair with yourself.

Overcome fear of not having needs met [this is more than financial] that drive you to imbalance on the mental level. There is much change on the horizon around you on ALL levels, as well as the potential for change within. Be aware that these can be very challenging, yet you are up to the challenge if you choose.

You must release those hidden fears and concerns that fill and cloud your mind, though you hesitate to speak of them. Those [are the] very ones [that] hold you back the most from deep enjoyment of life and from attaining the true purpose of human incarnation--which is Ascension. Rising to simply loving [the understanding being here, uncluttered by judgement].

Compassionate detachment is merely (nothing but) Divine Love in action!

God calls to you ELIZABETH. How do you answer?

And it is your divine duty to lift others spiritually. You have also acted to make this your physical pursuit. Integrity here means walking ahead of those you would teach, for as far as you can. How may you speak of a country with knowledge unless you have yourself explored it? You are not a signpost, nor a channeler of words! You are a leader--if you continue to so choose. One who leads must know the way themselves, or lead no more. [The emphasis here was strong and, because you commented on integrity after the reading, they have now asked that you contemplate these words and see that ALL integrity as a teacher is contained within the meaning conveyed here. In whomever you have discovered lack of integrity or where such is questionable, ask yourself whether they heed these words or not.]

Spirit awaits you--step in and face your emotional and mental chaos. Bring order to these, and only then can you truly rise and lead.

Your spiritual resources are [always] abundant. It is your responsibility to increase your emotional resources, as confusion muddies the mental water.

Turn to meditation to bring necessary control. Remove constraining beliefs. The sense of tiredness and overwhelm will dissolve as you make the time to spiritually connect. Take the time away from everyone and everything now to calm and still emotion and mind. Be reminded that your service is vital for the times to come--but only if you have trained your ears to hear the Voice of God!

Look around and truly see your physical security.

It is not necessary to wonder if you will be taken care of. This is your present reality! Financially and physically you ARE secure. ACT from the reality that you have worked for and accomplished, not from fear about your ability to attain more in the future.

Appreciating what you have achieved is NOT the same as resting on your laurels. It is a platform for strong action! Internal first and then external, within yourself and then with others. Do you wonder where you fit in this world? Quietly listen to the Angels, knowing that you fit always and perfectly in the arms of the Divine Mother!

Look truthfully within. Uncover any fear you have of being content. Learn its origin and release it at last. It does not belong to you!

Fill your heart and mind with joy, laughter and contentment, fully knowing that this will lead you to more of the same in all ways. [Here they explain that joy always leads to greater joy. What else can?] Contentment is not complacency. You will [in this way] always discover more! The difference is that you will have the peace of heart and mind to enjoy and appreciate it in every moment.

Physical success is yours. Now let this knowing free you to work to open your heart to God.

Remember that while we must work to care for our physical self, it [the physical self] is not the source of true security! Look at and learn from your parent's situation. Learn, Elizabeth! These Masters you call parents play out this lesson for your benefit as well as their own!

Spirit offers these lessons for your growth, but it is you who must choose to recognize them, learn and grow. Practice your faith, walk your talk and enjoy the resulting miracles!

Master these, for they are the ones you selected for this lifetime.

What is learned will then be taught--but not merely in a classroom but also from Your every breath others will draw inspiration, though you speak not a word.

Make time for Laughter in every day . . .for the Joy of simply Being. Those who see you will vibrate the same with you. This is the greatest Miracle."

Archangel Michael and Gabriel speak.

Chapter 24

LIFE LESSONS

E ARTH IS A NEUTRAL playing ground for us to work on our divine lessons for the soul. In difficult times, it can be hard to imagine that we really did sign up for this! Yet, we did, because it is here that we can advance our own knowledge and experience. And we are each given special teachers who bring us wonderful gifts and lessons to enhance our soul growth.

While it's easy to view angels and archangels, guides and masters as teachers, our friends and colleagues, our parents and children are teachers as well.

In fact, every situation and encounter is an opportunity to learn as well as teach, and it's up to us to recognize them.

The main spiritual teachers in this lifetime for me are my parents.

For years I have struggled with low self-esteem and learning to love and trust myself. I always looked for love outside of myself. I looked for it everywhere but inside of me. I was always behind in school and in emotionally maturing as a young girl. I had issues with my body image and for the most part, I did not feel like I fit in anywhere.

My parents, bless their hearts, tried to be the best parents that they could based on their own up-bringing. Both of my parents came from large families where there was much fighting and not a whole lot of love. The households were devoid of love and support.

Thus, this was the environment that I too was brought up in.

My father trusts no one and shares with no one. He is a very intelligent man who attended college but never believed in himself. He ended up working his whole life in a factory with no desire to succeed or move beyond. He had several opportunities to move up the ladder in the company that he worked for. But fearful of change and responsibility, he declined each time the offer was made.

He has two wonderful children but never knew how to enjoy them or enjoy life.

He is weak in spirit, a man with no dreams or goals who continues to live in fear and mistrust and has no friends. He lives alone and will probably leave this world alone.

Different from my father, my mother has goals and dreams.

In her younger days, she was a bit of an adventurer in the sense of her willingness to try out different things. She was always willing to experience new things and she was somewhat intuitive, which helped her in being a mom. She always knew when my brother and I were getting into trouble.

She is very religious, going to church faithfully every week. Although, strong-willed, with a powerful ego, she is weak in listening to spirit and has not learned to master that ego so that she can discern and follow the voice of God and angels.

My parents, predictably enough, divorced long ago, and my father lives at the Veterans Home in New Hampshire. His finances are limited and, when he lived by himself, he did not have the very best of things. Even his car was quite run down and was held together by duct tape. He never likes to try anything new or different, not even an idea. My father lives in stagnation. So with the opportunity of having a very fruitful life and abundance and happiness, he chose for himself a very different path, one that is devoid of love.

My mother, on the other hand, is just the opposite. She lives in the house that I was brought up in, which she has improved and updated over the years. She drives a Cadillac and changes her car about every two to three years. She loves the finer things in life like champagne, diamonds and all the things that success can bring. She is full of energy and sometimes even I have a hard time keeping up with her. She is in the world and of the world, and materialism is vital to her in evaluating others.

Living in the luxury of her lovely home, her fears convince her that she is only here to work and that there are no spiritual lessons for her. In her busyness, she brings chaos and drama, preventing herself from making her own spiritual connection.

Both parents have health issues that truly reflect their personal and spiritual challenges. My father has hypertension, gout, skin cancer and severe arthritis and eye and hearing difficulties.

My mother has skin cancer, hypertension, hearing loss and now macular degeneration and considered legally blind.

All of this makes sense. In my father, cancer represents the lack of self-love. The gout is about being impatient and holding much anger inside. The arthritis is the physical manifestation of someone who is not willing to be flexible, and his hearing and vision difficulties are about not wanting to listen or look at himself.

In my mother, the hypertension represents long standing unresolved emotional issues and even some hidden anger. Her loss of hearing and vision is no surprise. Her hearing difficulty is her unwillingness to hear her own inner voice and the voice of spirit. Because of her inability to look at herself more deeply and look at things in a spiritual way, her body may be taking away these gifts in order to force her to look at herself. Sadly she has so far made no changes in her behavior or her thinking. She is allowing only fear and anger to rule her decision making and her life.

Though my parents are very different, both struggle with the same lesson. They have karma with each other and have come together to work out their issues and to move on.

Coming from two opposite ends, both have missed their lesson on Love.

Even so, within all the heartache they have brought me, there are perfect life lessons, which these grand souls are allowing me to experience!

For this I am deeply, eternally grateful.

When I see with my spiritual eyes, I am able to rise above the difficulties and avoid repeating their mistakes.

With all its beauty and challenges, Earth is indeed here for us to gain experience, and learn divine lessons.

For some, it may be a lesson about patience. For others, truth and trust.

All of the lessons boil down to one basic lesson, which is Love.

Chapter 25

CHALLENGING MOMENTS

S PIRITUAL TEACHING WAS NOT something that I
even considered while growing up. However, because
of my soul contract, here I am teaching about angels and
other spiritual topics.

Being a spiritual teacher has been very exciting and
enlightening. However, it can be very challenging as well
as sometimes disheartening.

You see, while I am teaching and in front of the class, I
am truly blessed because I get to see the spiritual light bulbs
going on. It is quite clear during the classes and workshops
that many are having those "ah ha" moments. They are
starting to remember who they truly are and to know of the
power that they are. There is remembrance on many different levels and even seeing purpose in their life.

Even when I do angel readings, I am blessed with the
opportunity to see a soul's path and journey and to bear
witness to their own struggles and growth: celebrating with
them through all of their own lessons and see them step

into their own power. What a wonderful gift and blessing this is.

For the most part, teaching is quite rewarding and it does have its moments.

Being in that teacher or leader role, you always need to be aware of your actions and your intentions. I like to think of myself as being very fair and open and available to students and clients however, I did need to learn boundaries and sometimes saying "no." This is something I still am working on. I always want to assist others on their path and to help solve all of their problems and be able to make everyone feel better.

There have been times when I have helped some of my angel and Reiki students with networking and assisting them in locating a place to set-up their spiritual practice.

Even with pure intention in assisting them, I was taking on too much responsibility for their own growth and success. Of course I would love to see all of my students with a full practice, moving ahead with their spiritual path and helping many. But I needed to draw the line.

With the good intentions that I held for others and myself, I was discovering that as I offered to assist, many began to take advantage of me and my connections. Many placed me in the role of being their marketing agent, which only fostered a dependency on me for students and referrals.

With a firm "No," I had to stand my ground. I felt badly about needing to do this, but knew if this continued, I would be repeating the past. Because I have always felt different and not fitting in with the rest of the world, at a young age I felt the need to please everyone just to make a friend or to feel like I belonged.

Furthermore, while trying to assist many, I found myself quickly falling behind in my own work and becoming quite

140

distracted with the dramas of others. I also did not realize nor understood the lesson that came next.

There are some that have studied with me as well as with others and have taken their spirituality and their path very seriously. There are still many others who are actually doing their spiritual work through healing and energy work, teaching various topics and providing intuitive spiritual readings and counseling services.

Some deeply inspired even from their own readings and inner guidance, ushered in new possibilities that could help change the world. A small group of students got together and became very active in their own town and region in the area of Special Education/Children's issues and helped to educate parents and the community.

This is so beautiful and heart warming. However, there is another side to being that spiritual teacher and leader.

It has been very painful at times to watch very gifted souls who have much healing potential and have the ability to be a strong spiritual teacher and leader just close their eyes and go back to sleep. They have deliberately chosen to close their minds and hearts to the voice of God and their own soul.

I remember one particular incident where a student who gave beautiful angel readings contacted me and said that she was struggling too hard and that walking the path of mastery was too challenging.

The first time this happened, I talked to her about the meaning of her work. I worked with her to help her see through her own illusions. I counseled and even tried to open some other doors for her to make it more simple and easy.

At first it seemed to work. She began to see the angels again and her readings took off and all seemed well.

In the process, I was also learning that I was taking the paths of others too personally. I felt like they were rejecting me if they wanted to throw in the towel.

The listening, talking and brain storming worked for a little while. But, in this context, I came to realize it was nothing more than a Band-Aid fix and I needed to honor each soul's path even if I did not agree.

When a few more months passed, this gifted student contacted me by email saying that she did not feel like she belonged in the angel group with which she studied. She said, "Life remains too hard and walking this path is too difficult." She wanted to just simplify her life and return to her former life. No more angels or studying or paths of mastery. She just wanted a plain and simple life with no extra responsibility.

As I read her email, my heart sank and as I began to respond by saying some of the same things I had said before, I could feel Archangel Michael standing right beside me.

He spoke in a very loving and firm way. "Wish them blessings and leave the door open. Allow each to walk their own path even if you do not approve. Release this burden and let it go. It is not for you to hold on to and it is not your responsibility." Then in a flash Michael was gone.

My email reply was short and simple. I wrote, "I wish you well on your path and if you ever change your mind, just know that the door is open for you. Be well and Godspeed-Elizabeth."

It hurt to send this but I understood Michael's message. I never heard back from that person and I do hope she is doing well and has found her inner peace.

My challenge of being a spiritual teacher and leader is to allow each and every soul to walk its own path no matter what path they choose and honor that path.

Chapter 26

SYNCHRONISTIC
MESSAGES OF LOVE

W E RECEIVE MESSAGES OF love all the time from God, angels, our guides and the masters of Light. But do we listen and hear their messages?

Communication is always happening, and their messages of love can come in many different ways such as a license plate, number sequences, bumper stickers and street signs or a song on the radio.

Sometimes deep and poignant life altering messages come through strangers, and "out of the mouths of babes."

How very often parents have shared with me deep messages spoken easily and playfully by their children. Messages that remind us to rediscover the Joy and Love that is the true purpose of Life.

Even an animal or insect can open us to hearing God!

One day, after teaching a class in my home, I was tidying

up things in my living room, and noticed an ant right in the middle of my living room. The ant was injured and was struggling to move. I guess it might have been stepped on.

Being compassionate about nature, animals and even bugs, I gently picked the ant up and brought it some water and a little honey. I thought may be some food and nourishment would be in order and I treated this small creation with great love and compassion. If others saw me fussing over this ant, they would think that I was crazy!

Yet in that moment, I received the most beautiful and powerful message of all.

I suddenly heard in my mind, "Treat others with the same amount of love and compassion as you did this small creature." This message of love was simple and yet profound.

God and the heavens talk to us all the time and constantly through Divine synchronistic messages and events.

One evening, I was on my way home from teaching in Worcester, Massachusetts and, being alone, I started a conversation with Jesus in the car. Driving down the busy highway to one of my favorite restaurants, I asked Jesus to give me a clear concrete sign today if he was truly listening to me.

A bit later on, I noticed a pick-up truck that had an extra mud flap but it wasn't around or even near any of the tires. It was smack right in the middle of the back of the truck and the only thing written on it was "Jesus." I first thought that maybe Jesus was the name of the company because this was a commercial vehicle. However, as I drove up closer and around to the side of the truck, it was indeed a painting company but with an entirely different name. Hmmm.... I wonder if just may be Jesus was letting me know that he really was listening?

Another time I was very stressed out at my regular clinical job, so on my way to work, I asked the angels to please surround me with extra love and light that day and to please give me a clear sign that they were around me. I was in need of some extra tender loving care (TLC) and sure enough just within a few minutes of asking, a car literally pulled in front of me and I was guided to glance at the license plate, which was 444XC.

I quickly remembered from one of my angel books, that 444 means that the angels are surrounding and giving you extra support and love. I just had to laugh at this one.

Speaking of numbers, the number 555 means that big changes are coming so hold on you're going for a ride. I have been seeing this number sequence for quite some time now and each time, change of some kind has certainly followed.

I have gotten this message with the numbers on license plates, clocks, odometers, paid receipts and change, building numbers and on television.

I even found it once on my caller id as I checked for messages!

There it was- the number that was left "555-555-5555."

I was so stunned that I could not even think. How weird was this I thought.

I did call that number and sure enough it is not a working number. Not surprised by this, but what a powerful message with the numbers.

Now I always pay attention to the numbers and especially the 555's. Heads up! Change is coming!

I recall other 'heads up' messages that have come through friends.

For example, in early fall of 2002 I took a medical intuition class with a very gifted intuitive. A friend had phoned me about the class and asked me to go with her. I had no idea what I'd be getting into. So I said, "Sure, I would love to go."

The class was three weeks long, very interesting and expanded my own awareness, pushing my intuitive gifts to the limit.

On the last day of class, students had to do a medical reading on each other. So my friend and I partnered up.

While she scanned me with her eyes closed and feeling my aura, she suddenly opened her eyes wide and said, "Elizabeth, you have a new angel coming to you." I was quite surprised at her reaction and the message. I asked if this angel was a new spirit guide. "No!" she said "Elizabeth, there is a new angel that is coming to work with you." I thought to my self that she must have gotten the message confused, as I was not aware of any "new angel" that was trying to make it self known to me. I just laughed a little and brushed it off.

It was late, but on the way home after class, I decided to stop at the grocery store to pick up a few things. I arrived just 5 minutes before the store was closing.

There were only two other cars in the parking lot and as I stepped out of the car, I was drawn to look at the license plates. On the car to my left, the plate read 444LKB. The car to my right just had printed on it "ARIEL."

"Oh my God," I said to myself. "This is the new angel that is trying to get my attention and work with me!"

Archangel Ariel is a very powerful archangel. Her energy and color is a soft lilac or purple. She comes around when someone is getting ready to pursue a strong spiritual path but has blockages like self-esteem issues, worthiness and deservingness and even some self-sabotaging behaviors preventing him or her from their spiritual work.

Still in disbelief and just shaking my head, I ran into the store to make my purchases. I must have run too fast because the next morning I realized that I forgot a couple of items that I needed.

While getting ready to venture out to the grocery store again, I called on Archangel Ariel and I asked her, "Archangel Ariel if you are truly the new angel that I need to work with now, please give me a clear concrete sign today."

Off to the grocery store I went, not knowing what to expect. Just as before, I pulled into a space not really paying attention to anything around me.

However, when I jumped out of the car, my attention was drawn to the car parked two cars away from me.

And? You guessed it! It was the same car that I saw the other evening and the license of "ARIEL."

Of course, I began to work with Archangel Ariel to clear through some of my own personal blockages so that I could get myself moving even in a more powerful way.

When you ask for a sign, watch out because you will see sign after sign after sign.

I once found myself driving home from Vermont in a blizzard, wanting only to get home safe and sound. The snow was piling up quickly making the roads very slick. I made it up the ramp for getting on the highway and I knew I had to just keep going or else I would become stuck in the snow and ice.

I asked for angelic help and started to pull on to the highway. Everything was fine for the first couple of seconds. Then I began to spin out of control and heading in the opposite direction. A pick-up truck was coming my way and was headed right for me. I knew that the truck would not be able to stop in time and maneuvering around my car was limited.

With what could only have been Divine intervention, the truck saw me in time and somehow was able to quickly maneuver around me without incident. We were both just fine and I was able to get control over my car and headed back in the right direction.

Driving even more cautiously and slowly, I asked the Divine Mother to surround me in her loving arms and energy for a safe journey back home. As I spoke to her about my concerns and what I needed, I asked her to give me a sign that she was right here with me.

With snow and ice falling fast and heavy and piling up even faster with no plow or salt truck in sight, I could feel my car swerving on the road. Willing myself to remain calm and be still, I kept asking for help to get home safe and some kind of sign to reassure me.

I wasn't sure just how Divine Mother would do this, but She did it, perfectly as always!

Out of nowhere, I suddenly could see another small pick-up truck in front of me. My windshield was getting fogged up but I could make out the license plate which spelled 'MOTHER." I laughed and felt reassured that everything was going to be just fine, and it was. It took four hours but I got home without further incident, with the feeling of much gratitude.

I've shared a few of my own experiences, and indeed I feel truly blessed.

Yet, working as I do with people who are awakening and so actively opening their awareness to the many ways that God speaks to us, I know for certain that we all receive these messages of validation, confirmation and reassurance.

The Divine and the angels all have a wonderful sense of humor. They give us wonderful messages of hope and yes of love if we take the time to observe and listen.

It is always about Love and nothing more. We are here to remember the Love that we are and that Love leads us closer to our journey back home.

Chapter 27

MY JOURNEY BACK HOME

I T HAS BEEN AN interesting journey back home, of remembering who I am.

During my spiritual growth and development, I've learned that I need to continually work on myself for I am really my first client and one who needs healing the most. My angels were and are always right by my side lovingly guiding and supporting my every move.

When you start on your true spiritual path, different parts of your life begin to shift and change. I had to understand and accept that at times walking one's path may be a very lonesome road.

Many of the personal friends who have been in my life for several years are now gone because they do not understand what I do and they do not resonate with me anymore.

As sad as I have been to see this happen, I bless and release these relationships and have been gifted abundantly with deep, true and precious friends who celebrate my growth.

Now I understand and realize that my life purpose is to be a Lightworker and more specifically a spiritual teacher and healer. As I began walking on my spiritual path, I started to notice changes in the way I see situations and in the ways in which I handle my emotions, as well as the resulting changes in my aura. The spiritual classes I am guided to take help me to expand my Divine awareness and direction.

Over time, I knew that I was being guided to help others on a spiritual level. I know without any doubt that heaven is watching over me. I know at the soul level that I am a brave soul and that I am growing and evolving all the time. Change is inevitable and the angels shower me with confidence and guidance to keep me moving ahead.

I have felt and heard God's voice speak to me in my thoughts without a word being uttered, in a song I hear or perhaps in the laughter of an innocent child. In the music of nature from the wind blowing to the birds singing their love calls and seeing magical flight of the butterfly. Sometimes it is by the touch of a gentle unseen hand or presence especially when I am feeling low, sad and all alone. Sometimes I can hear God's voice in my quiet space when I ask for guidance and receive an answer. Or in my healing work when I see a person for the beautiful divine spirit that they are with the Unconditional Love of Oneness.

I didn't have to jump through hoops or do anything special to hear and make that connection. All I have to do is be. Being still, centered and quiet allows for my own connection. Just learning to be is of great importance to all, especially for lightworkers.

One can hear God speak by listening to the voice that comes from within our hearts. It does not need to come from anywhere else or anyone else or anything else.

I have found Gods words in my own heart. The Divine speaks to all but it is we who choose to listen or not. Some believe that they have to be at a certain spiritual level to make the connection happen. Others believe that they need someone else to make the connection for them or that they need certain oils, innocence, healing tools and mantras. In truth, you don't need all of these things. You are your own Divine tool!

The truth and power of having that connection is Divine Love. The connection to God is in all things and it is up to us to choose to either feel connected or separate from Source.

As a lightworker, I have consciously chosen to live my soul contract through the life I live and the work that I do. I have chosen to remember that connection and use it daily. Is it easy to live Love, Compassion, and Kindness daily? No, but it is my daily goal and one that I am committed to and coming closer to each and every day.

I have become very determined and disciplined so that I may assist others to discover their own Divinity and inner truth, to bring out the very best and empower themselves.

I must be constantly aware of my dependency of looking outside of myself for validation of self-worth, success and love and not allowing fear to rule or influence my decisions and perceptions. I had to learn to face my fear and even partnership with my fear to turn fear into a creative force that can be used positively.

Stubbornness is still a challenge for me. As I strive to be more flexible and open to change, I free myself.

I am not PERFECT! But my deep spiritual awakening has led me to be aware of my challenges or traps. The bringing together of the sum of my human/spiritual existence was necessary for me to stay focused on my path and continue the spiritual work that I had embarked on.

While working on this book, I asked Archangel Michael to assist me with a channeled message. The italicized writing is what Archangel Michael wanted to share.

"I am here with you. Thank you for bringing others to the light, God is very pleased.

Your true self is made up of pure light and you radiate much love—Divine love. You as a healer will be perfectly guided and have a firm foundation to build on. You are very powerful and will bring much joy to many who come in contact with you. Your treatment modality is almost complete. What I mean is that you need to keep working on your self, trust, and love. You are greatly supported in your endeavors and we will be here at your beckoned call.

You will help make a difference and you will bring many to the light and will help others to see us. For you have already done so. You know what we mean. Trust in yourself and you will be healed. We need people like you to help the angelic realm and to help with the energy change that is occurring. Do you understand? You will bring peace where there is discord. You will bring love where there is hate and anger. You will help to heal. Fear of Love is what is keeping you from fully being who you are and need to evolve into. Don't be afraid—trust, and trust the love.

Use all of your talents and gifts. Listen to the inner voice way deep inside you—just listen and sense our presence. We are very real and with you all the time. Never fear that we will leave you stranded and alone. Be at peace my little child. You are dearly loved—Michael.

I hope you enjoyed reading this book and that just maybe my story has touched you and maybe even awakened you to your own divinity.

When you answer your Divine calling, you can never fail or fall short of any expectations!

Enjoy your awakening and journey back home!

APPENDIX

REQUESTING ANGELIC
HELP AND SUPPORT

YOUR SPIRITUAL TEAM IS just a shout away. If you feel more comfortable talking with God that is fine. But do know that you also have angels and there are masters who are around to also assist and provide comfort, support and guidance.

Just by either thinking or saying out loud "Angels I Need Help," your spiritual team gathers all around you.

If you feel more comfortable writing, you can write a letter to your angels and just be honest with your feelings and explain your situation that you need assistance with.

Prayer is a form of asking for something and meditation is about listening to our Divine guidance. So you can pray for guidance and then take the time to listen for their loving response back to you. Since we live in a world of duality, it is important to remember to always attach your prayers to God's Will. I ask that these prayers are in perfect alignment with the Will of God because there is no duality in God's Will.

You can also invite them into your dreams at night. Just state your intention before you go to sleep and give your angels permission to work with you and on you during your dream time. They will be glad to assist in any way and remember to journal your dreams in the morning.

Asking for a sign is a wonderful way to receive validation that God and the Angels are hearing your requests and they may even make their presence known to you through signs. They may either give you an appropriate sign or you can ask for a specific sign. One time I asked Mother Mary to give me a heart shaped rock that will signify that she is around, and low and behold, I received one shortly after asking. They do understand that from time to time we have trouble trusting, so if you need a sign to validate their presence in your life or help with a situation, just ask.

Lastly, when your faith in yourself or in God and the angels needs to be strengthened, all you have to do is ask for more faith. Archangel Michael is wonderful at infusing us with more faith in ourselves and in our spiritual team.

ARCHANGELS

THE ARCHANGELS SEEM MUCH bigger in size than your guardian angels and they all have their specialty. Here are the eight most popular archangels and their gifts and area of specialty.

Archangel Ariel: Her name means, "lion of God" and her energy is a soft pale purple or lilac. Ariel is a very strong and powerful yet gentle archangel. She is also one of the angels of the healing ray and her specialty is healing negative self-talk and self-sabotaging behavior. She has the ability to heal you and help you spread your wings so you can soar with your dreams and visions. She can support you by helping you to stand in your power and give you the courage to make changes in your life. When you are ready to take a leap of faith but you lack faith within yourself, invoke Ariel and ask her to help you to do your soul mission work with full faith and support.

Archangel Azrael: His name means, "whom God helps" and his energy is a pale white color. He is best known as one of the angels who greets and safely escorts deceased loved ones over to the other side by assisting the soul in separating from the body. Azrael also specializes in helping Lightworkers with mediumship. Mediumship means connecting with the spirit world and receiving messages, information and validation from deceased loved ones. Call on Azrael when your departing loved ones need to have a safe and comfortable transition or if you are being called to develop your mediumship ability.

Archangel Gabriel: Her name means, "hero of God or God is my strength" and her energy is a bright gold color. Gabriel is one of the three prominent angels of Christianity along with Michael and Raphael. There is some controversy about the nature of this archangel. Some experience Gabriel to be more of a male energy and some feel Gabriel to be of a female energy and some even called Gabriel, Gabrielle. Whatever your experience is, know that it is perfect for you. This archangel is one of the angels who best serves creativity, speaking and communication, business and networking. Gabriel is the messenger angel and works with those aspiring to be teachers, artisans, writers and world leaders. Call upon Gabriel to guide you and inspire you with creative thoughts, lead by empowerment and empowering others and speaking your truth with love and compassion or starting a new project or career.

Archangel Jophiel: Her name means, "beauty of God" and her energy is pink. Jophiel helps you to see the bigger picture from a spiritual point of view. Jophiel is mentioned as being the angel who drove Adam and Eve out from the

Garden of Eden after they ate the fruit from the Tree of Life. Therefore, Jophiel helps with exposing injustices and corruption and can bring the truth out in a situation or person. She helps you to see with clear perception, knowledge and Divine wisdom. When your questioning the integrity of a person or situation, call on Jophiel to help you see the truth and turn knowledge into wisdom.

Archangel Metatron: His name means, "Angel of the Presence." From Greek Meta + Tron means Beyond + Matrix and Metatron is a reference to the highest archangel. He is referred to as "King of the Angels" and is the only archangel who once walked upon the earth as a man (as the prophet Enoch) and is brother to Archangel Sandalphon. His energy is very striking and is almost like that of a watermelon (pink and green). He brings spiritual awareness, understanding and knowledge to anyone who asks. He is considered the intermediary link between God and humanity or the Divine and the human. Biblical history records that after Exodus, Metatron guided the children of Israel to safety. He is often seen as working with Mother Mary to help children of the new Earth. Another specialty of Metatron is regulating energy. He helps to regulate the light energies and frequencies that we are absorbing and works with sacred geometry (Metatron Cube which is the foundation to all matter) to help clear and balance chakras. If you are feeling over-whelmed by energy or having energy work performed on you, call him in to work with you and the energy healer to help adjust the energies around you so that you are perfectly balanced.

Archangel Michael: His name means, "he who is as God" or "he who looks like God" and his energy can be seen as a cobalt blue or a bluish purple color. Michael holds a blue flaming sword of love that he uses to free us from lower entities and entanglements. He is by far the most famous archangel and most popular among Lightworkers. Michael has an ability of eliminating fear, anxiety and negativity in our lives. He gives us the courage and energy to make changes in our lives and helps us to fulfill our mission on Earth. He is also the protector and can give you more faith in yourself and in your spiritual allies. Michael is able to transmute and transform negative, destructive or hate-filled energies and can clear out stagnant and negative energy from our energy field or aura as well as from our home, office and vehicle. If you are bothered with earth bound spirits, invoke the energy of Michael to surround you and to quickly escort the spirits back to the light. When disturbing nightmares occur, invite Michael to clear you and not be afraid. Call on Michael if you feel afraid, anxious, having courage to make changes, increasing your level of faith or needing clarity of your life-purpose path. When you feel like a victim, ask Michael to help you become the victor.

Archangel Raphael: His name means, "God heals" and the color of Raphael's energy is an emerald green. He is in charge of physical healing of this planet and all its' inhabitants. He inspires and guides all those who are called to the healing profession (traditional or alternative healing) and can guide you to the most appropriate healing programs and modalities and even assists with new cures. If you are a healer, invite Raphael to join you and to assist you with the healing session. Raphael can easily work with you and your medical team and can even help you locate the most perfect healer, physician and dentist for you. Call on Raphael if you need physical healing of yourself or another, aid in healing animals, needing support during your medical challenges and guide you on the right healing career path.

Archangel Uriel: His name means, "God is my light" and his energy is a soft pale yellow. He is the psychologist angel and helps to heal heart wounds and old unforgiveness and aids in bringing peace and harmony back into a relationship. When you need assistance in healing anger, resentment or bitterness in relationships or situations, call on Uriel, he will quickly answer your call and enlighten you to the solution of your challenge and help heal your heart and mind.

ASCENDED MASTERS

ASCENDED MASTERS ARE HIGHLY evolved beings of light who once lived on this Earth plane. They have fulfilled their divine plan and have ascended into the presence of the Divine. They reside in the spirit world and have made a commitment to assisting those who are serious about their spiritual path and the ascension path. Each Master has chosen a dominant energetic quality to infuse into their presence and range of experience and expertise.

Here are the ten most popular Masters of our time; Athena, El Morya, Hilarion, Jesus the Christ, Kuthumi, Melchizedek, Mother Mary, Quan Yin, Saint Germaine and Serapis Bey.

Athena—her full name is Pallas Athena is a Greek goddess and a powerful master indeed. She is referred to as the warrior goddess who uses wisdom and words like a sword. She had lifetimes back in Lemuria and Atlantis. She was one of the High Priestess in Atlantis working in the Temple of

Truth. Truth, integrity, protection, writing, speaking your truth and holding your own power are areas of her specialty. Call on her when these are needed for yourself or a situation that you find yourself in.

El Morya—in some past incarnations was Abraham, one of the Three Wise Men at the birth of the Christ child, King Solomon and King Arthur of the legend of Camelot. His energy reminds you of a very strict and loving father. He is a stern master who is mostly noted for his devotion to God and deep commitment to the Divine Plan. El Morya represents the Will of God and makes sure that God's Will be done with perfection. He is the Master of Universal Laws and truth and is the defender of justice. If you need assistance in understanding and working with universal laws or needing more personal or spiritual discipline, call on El Morya.

Hilarion—known as the master physician and healer and his focus is on health, healing and science. He is noted as being one of the apostles to Jesus, Apostle Paul. He works in a similar way to Archangel Raphael, the healing angel, and can assist with healing our physical body. His mental power and focus is very strong making it possible for new scientific developments and medical breakthroughs. He can further assist individuals with controlling their mental thoughts and can guide an individual with their spiritual development.

Jesus the Christ—also called Sananada or the Most Radiant One and is the archetype of God's identity. According to Edgar Cayce, he claims that Jesus was also Adam, Enoch, Jeshua, Joshua and Joseph of Egypt. Jesus was one of the

High Priests in the Order of Melchizedek and is part of the Holy Trinity. He is the master of forgiveness and healing and is the ultimate role model for humanity. When you need more faith, wanting a clearer channel to God, forgiveness, healing and miracles call on Jesus to assist you in these areas.

Kuthumi—he is considered to be the World Teacher and has a large ashram of students and holds the Office of the Christ with Jesus (the office of the 144,000 Masters). In the past, he was one of the Three Wise Men at the birth site of Jesus and also took embodiment as John the Beloved, a favorite apostle to Jesus. His role is to bring enlightenment through education and anyone aspiring to be a teacher or to have a deeper spiritual understanding, Kuthumi is a wonderful spiritual mentor and teacher.

Melchizedek—referred to as the Eternal Lord of Light and is charged with overseeing and directing the cosmos in preparing Earth for the Fifth Dimension. He heads the command and Order of Melchizedek which oversees the Masters of Light who work with humanity in bringing illumination, ancient knowledge and wisdom. Many of the Ascended Masters has lineage to the Order of Melchizedek, which is comprised of high priests and priestesses. When you need a greater understanding of spiritual or esoteric information, deeper insight and wisdom, protection from psychic attacks and spirit entity attachments, call on Melchizedek.

Mother Mary—referred to as the Virgin Mary and also called Queen of the Heavens or Queen of the Angels. Mary is the mother of Jesus and is a powerful feminine energy who holds great power in manifesting miracles and is a champion and defender and protector of children. She also has a special talent of bringing couples together and assisting them in starting a family. Her gift is compassion and bringing in Divine Love. Anyone who desires to be a more loving parent or works with children or wants to be more loving and nurturing, needing assistance with their love life, call on Mother Mary for her wisdom and love.

Quan Yin—often referred to as the Goddess of Mercy and Compassion and sometimes called the "Mother Mary of the East." Master Quan Yin had numerous incarnations prior to her ascension and she has promised to teach the children of God how to balance their karma and fulfill their Divine plan and to be infused with the Christ Consciousness energy. Her greatest gift to humanity is mercy and she provides this through her ability to love unconditionally. Call on Quan Yin when you need to be more open to giving and receiving love, being kinder to self and others and embody the energy of the Divine Mother.

Saint Germaine—his real name is Count of Saint-Germain or Comte de Saint-Germaine. He is the holder of the Violet Flame of transmutation. The Violet Flame is used to transmute any energy that is of a lower vibration to a higher one. In other incarnations, he was Joseph, the father to Jesus, Merlin in Camelot, the prophet Samuel and Francis Bacon just to name a few. He was involved in establishing secret societies and mystery schools and teaching alchemy. Legend has it that Saint Germaine could turn lead into gold among other things and is considered a great alchemist of our time. Ask Saint Germaine to teach you the ways of the Violet Flame and like Archangel Michael, the Violet Flame can clear you of stuck energy and even clear out negativity from your environment.

Serapis Bey—he is the Master of Ascension and is sometimes referred to as "the disciplinarian" because of his commitment to help others to take good care of their physical body and health. Call on Serapis Bey when you are seeking out information on the ascension process, needing more assistance on your spiritual path or need more motivation in taking good care of your physical body.

SPIRITUAL TOOLS
FOR THE SOUL

WHILE WALKING ON OUR path, we may encounter challenges, blockages and obstacles. Here are some spiritual tools for the soul, which are self-help tips. Know whom to call on for help with angel healing techniques for the soul.

Negativity

- Clearing Self and Environment (home, vehicle and/ or work) with Archangel Michael. Invoke Michael and ask him to clear you both inside and out and remove in all directions of time, space and dimension -all excess energy, negativity, Earth bound spirits, entities, lower vibrational energies and beings, psychic dirt debris and slime, parasites, and any entity, energy or being that is not from the light or has been reprogrammed by the

173

light or not 100% pure light, all devices and implants and negative elementals and any beacons of Light that is used for darkness or the opposing forces. Michael, take all of this back to the source of light from which it came! So be it and so it is done! Thank You Michael.

- Cutting Energy Cords with Archangel Michael. Sometimes people can become energetically attached to us and lower our energy and drain us. Just ask Archangel Michael to please use his blue flaming sword of love to cut away and dissolve in all directions of time and space all cords of attachment now and take them to the light as well. Thank you Michael.

- Clearing Aura in Shower using Rainbow Light. This is a very simple visualization whereby you need to set the intention first of clearing your aura in the shower. Then step into the shower and allow the shower water to hit the top of your head and see and feel the water cast down all around you and removing all the heavy energy and psychic dirt and debris. Visualize all of this just getting washed away. Make sure you do all sides, so do the front first and in a clockwise fashion, turn to your right and keep going. If you know how to scan energy, you can scan your sides to see if all the stuck heavy energy is gone. Whatever you remove you need to replace, this is a universal law. So now that the negative energy is gone, you can ask either your Higher Self, angels or the masters of light that you work with what color would be good or appropriate for you to work with now. Let's say you get the color purple. Infuse the shower water with purple light and energy and do all four sides again. You are putting more positive and spiritual energy back in.

- You can invoke the violet flame and run it right through your whole body and auric field. The violet flame of transmutation that changes anything from a lower or denser vibration and energy to one that is higher.

Anxiety

- Invoke Archangel Michael and tell him what you are afraid of or anxious about. Be very honest with him. Then if you feel comfortable enough, give Michael permission to enter your body and ask him to calm your body down and restore peace of mind and harmony. It works and you don't need a doctor's prescription.

- Heart Opening Exercise using White Light. This visualization is very powerful and even has empowering effects. Place yourself in a quiet state of mind and in a comfortable position. See in your mind's eye a door on your heart. See yourself walking up to the door and opening the door on your heart. Look inside and see white light everywhere. Now push the door wide open and allow the white light to flow out of your heart and into your own body. See and feel the white light permeating every single cell, organ and all of your tissues. See and feel the white light flowing through your whole body and even flowing out of your palms of your hands and soles of your feet. You are now just pure white light. Be in that energy and you will find yourself totally overcome by peace. When you feel that you have allowed enough of that energy to flow from your heart, just ask the energy to flow back into your heart space and know that it will always be there.

Chakra Clearing

- Call on Archangel Michael, Archangel Raphael and your guardian angels and tell them both that you want to do a deep cleansing of your chakras. While standing very tall and confidently, direct your guardian angels to stand in front of you with one on each side. See them holding a huge bucket and see the Violet Flame of Transmutation in the middle of the bucket. Ask Michael to stand in front of the bucket, he is only there to assist if assistance is needed. Archangel Raphael is standing to one of your sides and he has with him a canister almost like a fire extinguisher and it's filled with emerald green cleansing foam. Visualize all of this happening right now. Next, take your right hand and place it about 2-3 inches above your root chakra that sits at the base of your spine. In a counter-clockwise fashion (which means elbow goes out to the wall first) rotate your hand almost like your unscrewing a lid on a jar twelve times and then see yourself lifting off the cover of your root chakra. With your inner vision, see or sense if there is anything that needs or wants to come out. Some experience black sludge, mud, black water and even parasites like worms. Allow all of this to come out and see it going right into the violet flame. This is all transmuted and healed. When this chakra feels or looks clean, ask Raphael to step forward and hose the chakra with his emerald green cleansing foam and see the residual flow right into the golden bucket. Now the chakra is clear and clean. Again, whatever you remove you need to replace (It's that universal law thing), take your right hand and place it like you did before just 2-3 inches above your root chakra and without moving, see and feel liquid gold light pouring from your palm chakra and now filling completely your root chakra. Do all major seven chakras (root, sacral, solar plexus, heart, throat, third eye and crown) and direct your team to the back of you and ask them to the cleansing on the back of your root chakra, upper part of your back and back of neck. Afterward, you will feel peaceful and refreshed. After the deep cleansing of all the chakras has taken place, you may only need to occasionally do the deep cleansing or if only one or two chakras do not feel right, you can just do this clearing exercise on those chakras themselves.

Spiritual Safety and Protection

- Ask Archangel Michael to spread his wings all around you and put his armor and shield around you in all directions (north, south, east, west, above and below). You can put yourself in a white bubble of light and oil or slime the outside of the bubble. Anything that is a lower vibration and energy just slides right off. Then ask Archangel Michael and your guardian angels to surround you with golden light of protection.

- Use Warrior Angels by asking Archangel Michael to assign four large Warrior Angels (two male and two females-balance energy) one to the North, South, East and West to always guard and protect your home, everyone in your home including all pets or living things, and everything in the home right now and thank you!

Low Energy

- Call on Archangel Michael and your guardian angels to help lift your energy and mood, it's just that simple.

LIGHTWORKER'S JOURNAL

Date:

Reflection of Day:

Chakra Work:

Prayer Work:

Meditation Messages:

Gratitude Statement:

Daily Goal(s):

Action Plan for Goal(s):

Daily Affirmation:

Journal Messages:

LIGHTWORKER'S JOURNAL

Date:

Reflection of Day:

Chakra Work:

Prayer Work:

Meditation Messages:

Gratitude Statement:

Daily Goal(s):

Action Plan for Goal(s):

Daily Affirmation:

Journal Messages:

BOOK RESOURCES

Baba, Prem Raja. *The Joy Book*. Mount Shasta, CA: Prem Raja Baba, 1998.

Berg, Yehuda. *The Power of Kabbalah*. San Diego, CA: Jodere Group, Inc., 2001.

Braden, Gregg. *The Isaiah Effect*. New York, NY: Three Rivers Press, 2000.

Brown, Kenneth. *We Came as Angels*. Minnetonka, MN: Waterwoods Press, 2002.

Carroll, Lee. *The Journey Home*. Carlsbad, CA: Hay House, Inc., 1997.

Davidson, Gustav. *A Dictionary of Angels*. New York, NYL The Free Press, 1971.

Dyer, Wayne Dr. *Getting in the Gap*. Carlsbad, CA: Hay House, Inc., 2003.

Ferruolo, David. *Connecting with the Bliss of Life*. Laconia, NH: D. Michael Ferruolo Enterprises, 2005.

Guiley, Rosemary Ellen. *The Encyclopedia of Angels*. New York, NY: Checkmark Books, 2004.

Hanh, Thich Nhat. *Living Buddha, Living Christ*. New York, NY: Riverhead Books, 1995.

Hawkins, David. *Transcending the Levels of Consciousness*. W. Sedona, AZ: Veritas Publishing, 2006.

Holland, John. *Born Knowing*. Carlsbad, CA: Hay House Inc., 2003.

Melchizedek, Drunvalo. *Living in the Heart*. Flagstaff, AZ: Light Technology Publishing, 2003.

Milanovich, Norma Dr., McCune, Shirley Dr., *The Light Shall Set You Free*. Scottsdale, AZ: Athena Publishing, 1996.

O'Hanlon, R. *Pathways to Spirituality*. New York, NY: W.W. Norton & Company, 2006.

Page, Christine Dr. *Spiritual Alchemy*. United Kingdom: C.W. Daniel Company Limited, 2003.

Rother, Steve. *Spiritual Psychology*. Poway, CA: Lightworker, 2004.

Stone, Joshua David. *Soul Psychology*. New York, NY: Ballantine Wellspring Publishing, 1994.

Virtue, Doreen. *The Lightworker Way*. Carlsbad, CA: Hay House, Inc., 1997.

Virtue, Doreen, *Divine Guidance: How to Have a Dialogue with God and Your Guardian Angels*. Los Angeles, CA: Renaissance Books, 1998.

Walsh, Neale Donald. *Communion with God*. New York, NY: G.P. Putman's Sons, 2000.

Walsh, Neale Donald. *The New Revelations: A Conversation with God*. New York, NY: Atria Books, 2002.

Yogananda, Paramahansa. *Autobiography of a Yogi*. Los Angeles, CA: Self-Realization Fellowship. 1946.

ACKNOWLEDGEMENTS

I WOULD LIKE TO ACKNOWLEDGE Ally, an amazing friend and colleague I met at Angel Camp who witnessed my transformation, and lovingly mentored me on my journey. You, Ally, helped me through some dark nights of the soul and helped me to take my ideas and manifest them into reality. For this, I am deeply grateful to you and all of your support as well as your editing expertise.

To my parents, for without them, my soul lessons would not be so clear or fully understood. My parents even though very different from me, were indeed perfect parents for me on a soul level. I bless them both for the gifts and blessings that they have given me.

To Tracy, who was a spiritual inspiration while writing this book and for believing in my work.

For all the assistance I received in writing this, my first book, I want to thank my editor, Laureen Belleville, David Ferruolo, and Tom Campbell of King Printing for guiding me with their knowledge and wisdom of the publishing world.

Thank you to all of my students and clients who allowed me to share in a part of their own soul's journey and helped me to be a better teacher.

Special thanks to Renee Walsh, my angel assistant who kept me sane throughout this project and helped with the research and editing of this book.

Lastly, a special heart-felt gratitude to God, Archangel Michael, Archangel Gabriel and my Guardian Angels for all their love, patience and Divine guidance that I have received on my journey and in creating Angel Street Publishing and this book. I am forever grateful for your friendship, wisdom and the Divine synchronicities in my life.

ABOUT THE AUTHOR

ELIZABETH FOLEY, EDM, MPH, is an international Angelologist, Reiki Master, Integrated Energy Therapist and author. She is currently a doctoral candidate in Metaphysics at the American Institute of Holistic Theology.

She is a frequent guest speaker on various radio and television shows in the New England area. These have included the Liz Walker show on CBS/Channel 4, Univision Nueva Inglaterra and Planetary Spirit, an internet radio talk show which provides in-depth interviews on spirituality and living in awareness. She has also presented at the 2005 Berkshire Paranormal Conference and Seminar in North Adams, MA.

Elizabeth holds Master Degrees in both Counseling and Public Health from Boston University. She formerly enjoyed a successful career in the healthcare field with an emphasis on clinical research. She also spent more than 12 years in the pharmaceutical and biotechnology industry.

As owner of Divine Healing in Nashua NH, Elizabeth conducts private sessions as well as facilitates unique spiritual workshops and certification programs about Angels, Spirituality, Psychic Development and Soul Therapy.

For additional information about her workshops, certfication programs or lecture schedule, contact:

Elizabeth J. Foley
Divine Healing
P.O. Box 7124
Nashua, NH 03060
603-888-0658
www.divinehealing.us
divine_healing@worldnet.att.net

Hope you enjoyed this Angel Street Publishing book.
If you would like to view additional Angel Street
Publishing books and products,
please contact:

Angel Street Publishing, LLC
P.O. Box 7298
Nashua, NH 03060

www.angelstreetpublishing.net

ANGEL HEALING PRACTITIONER©
CERTIFICATE PROGRAM

The Angel Healing Practitioner© certification course encourages you to awaken your intuition, read energy, conduct angel readings confidently and learn and practice angel healing techniques. You will also discover ways in which the angelic realm communicates with you and learn to receive messages, information and Divine guidance from angels.

The main objective of the course is to:

- Teach you how to give accurate and healing angel readings, explore various card spreads and how to interpret the meaning of the cards.

- Help you discover your natural Divine communication style and how to combine clairvoyance, clairaudience, clairsentience and claircognizance with your card readings to gain deep insight and understanding.

- Learn about the angelic realm including information about your Guardian Angels, Archangels, Ascended Masters and Deceased Loved Ones.

- Teach you how to prepare yourself for conducting an angel session.

- Practice automatic writing with Archangel Michael for receiving messages and information.

- Learn and practice angel-healing techniques for self and others.

- Be aware of the ethical and confidentiality issues involved during an angel session.

- Learn techniques to build your practice.

For more information and dates, please contact Elizabeth J. Foley at Divine Healing, P.O. Box 7124, Nashua, NH 03060 or visit on line at www.divinehealing.us.

SOUL THERAPY PRACTITIONER©
CERTIFICATION PROGRAM

Each of us has a unique Divine soul and soul mission and the Soul Therapy Practitioner® (STP) Program is dedicated to an in-depth discovery, healing and clearing of the different aspects of your mental, emotional, physical and spiritual bodies. The goal of the STP program is to help you discover and align your inner spiritual life with your outer life and to empower yourself and others. In this powerful certification course, not only will you embark on your own inner sacred quest, but you also will learn how to assist others on their spiritual journey and discovery.

The Soul Therapy Practitioner® (STP) program is a four-month self-guided program and includes:

1. What is the Soul
2. Listening and Connecting to Your Soul
3. Understanding and Opening the Seven Seals (spiritual issues and the chakras)
4. The Seven Rays and How They Guide Your Soul
5. Development of the Soul (discovering your soul age, level and role)
6. Basics of Spiritual Psychology (exploring the twelve life lessons & creating a spiritual psychological profile)
7. Awakening and Clearing the Physical, Mental, Emotional and Spiritual Body
8. Tools for Emotional and Spiritual Healing
9. Steps to Attain Mastery and Manifest Your Mission

For more information and dates, please contact Elizabeth J. Foley at Divine Healing, P.O. Box 7124, Nashua, NH 03060 or visit on line at www.divinehealing.us.

RADIO SHOW
THE PHOENIX HOUR WITH ELIZABETH FOLEY
OF DIVINE HEALING

Tips and Tools for Personal and Spiritual Transformation.

Come and join us for an hour of metaphysical exploration and consciousness expansion. Each week there will be straight talk exploring various metaphysical theories, beliefs, healing modalities and tools for personal and spiritual transformation.
Be the Phoenix...forever changing and transforming.

Hosted by Elizabeth Foley, an international Angelologist, Metaphysician and Author. She will introduce some of the most outstanding names in metaphysics as well as some new emerging personalities in the spiritual community. Join her as she explores not only angels but everything else under the stars.

Listen "Live" to "The Phoenix Hour with Elizabeth Foley of Divine Healing" beginning January 9, 2008 every Wednesday (4 PM - 5 PM EST) on www.toginet.com. Call in with your questions and stories at: (877) 864-4869.

Visit www.divinehealing.us
or you can go on line to www.toginet.com
to see the full listing.to see schedule of speakers and topics.